GOLF
TECHNIQUES IN
PICTURES

Michael Brown

Book Consultant: Billy A. Williford, Jr.
Head Pro at University of North Carolina Finley Golf Course

D1401298

A Perigee Book

Perigee Books
are published by
The Putnam Publishing Group
200 Madison Avenue
New York, NY 10016

Library of Congress Cataloging-in-Publication Data

Brown, Michael, date.
    Golf techniques in pictures / Michael Brown; book consultant,
  Billy A. Williford, Jr.
        p.   cm.
    ISBN 0-399-51664-6 (alk. paper)
    1. Golf. I. Williford, Billy A. II. Title.
  GV965.B838   1991   90-22417 CIP
  796.352—dc20
                    Cover design by Lisa Amoroso
Front cover photograph © by Brian Drake/SportsChrome East-West
Printed in the United States of America
    3 4 5 6 7 8 9 10

This book is printed on acid-free paper.
∞

Contents

1. Introduction

This book is designed to be useful for novices and as a refresher course for more experienced golfers. It does not detail the *rules* of the sport, but rather it covers the fundamental *techniques* of golf that should be familiar to all good golfers. These basics are necessary to play a good game, and they help players enjoy the game, too. The book covers golf equipment, examines the swing, and then moves on to discuss the short game, putting rules, and tactics. It takes you in a chapter-by-chapter sequence down the road to better golf.

• •

More than 24 million people play golf in the United States, making it the most widely enjoyed outdoor sport in this country. There's good reason for its popularity—golf is a great game. It places you and your companions in beautiful, well-cared-for landscapes; it's relaxing and challenging; it stretches and strengthens the body while it stimulates the mind; it provides camaraderie and social activity. Also, golf is an accessible game. Unlike many sports, the physical requirements are not overwhelming. It can be played on the highest levels by all physical types.

Finally, one of golf's greatest qualities is that it is not a sport that must be given up with the passing of youth, but can be a lifetime activity for both men and women.

But, along with providing all these and other benefits, golf may also challenge your patience at times. For starters, a fundamentally sound golf swing is one prerequisite to enjoying the game. It is also one of the more difficult skills to master in all of sports. It is not a gift given to the athletically talented after a few swings, but the reward for long hours of diligent practice and careful thought and concentration.

I wish this book could be titled *Golf Made Simple,* but it can't. This book offers some simple, straightforward explanations and ways of approaching the game. But despite an outward appearance of simplicity, golf is not and cannot be rendered simple; it is not an easy game.

I also offer two challenges as you begin your journey—one concrete and one mental. The concrete challenge: Give yourself at least eighteen months of play *and* practice (with the help of a pro if you can afford it) before you decide whether golf is for you. If you do this, you will probably be a golfer for life. The mental challenge: As the months go by and you tackle various golfing challenges, you may become frustrated. If you find that happening, think back to your first day on the driving range, which was probably comically awful, and remind yourself of how far you have come. From that perspective, your sense of confidence—as well as the pleasure and enjoyment that should be the point of any recreation—will be greatly enhanced.

Finally, in order to allow the reader some pleasure in these pages of how-to, I have tried not to overload them with golf jargon. It would not be possible, or desirable, however, to avoid the language of golf altogether, some of which will be unfamiliar to the true novice. Rather than defining each golf term as we proceed, a glossary is provided at the back of this volume, which also includes various other terms that may stump you when you first hit the course.

2. Equipment

A well-executed drive off the tee is achievable if a golfer strives to keep the game as straightforward as possible. One way to do this is to first master those variables in your game that you can control. There are many things that you cannot totally control: your lie, the condition of the course, the tension you feel from your opponents. But you *can* control your choice of equipment.

It is vitally important that you have clubs of good quality that are suited to you. They are the only physical connection you have with the ball when it is in play.

First time out, rent some clubs and check with the pro to see that they fit. Later, if you want, buy a used set. Finding one should not be a problem. The vast majority of novice golfers will be perfectly well served with a well-made set of standard clubs (with perhaps some slight modification from the local pro). Learn to swing these clubs properly and then by all means trade up into a set of beautiful new sticks. After all, some people feel that using and taking care of fine tools is one of the great pleasures of golf.

So now, being very wary of the marketing hype associated with the sales of golfing equipment and accessories, let's talk about what you'll need to carry out onto the course.

Clubs

For a competitive round of golf, a golfer may choose up to fourteen clubs. The choices may come from woods, numbered 1–5; irons, usually numbered 1–9; a pitching wedge; and a sand wedge, all of which generally come in a matched set. A putter is also always included among the fourteen clubs, but preferences and criteria for putters are very individual and they are not included in matched sets.

If you are on a budget, you can start with a half set of clubs (clubs can be bought individually). A good beginner's half set would consist of a 3-wood, 3-iron, 5-iron, 7-iron, 9-iron, sand wedge, and putter.

Generally speaking, an experienced golfer with a full set of clubs will play a typical hole using the clubs in ascending order, starting with his 1-wood (or driver) for the tee shot, his second shot (from the fairway) using perhaps a 3-iron, and his third stroke, a 9-iron over a tree and onto the green. The fourth shot would require a sand wedge, since the golfer failed to put enough backspin on the ball and it rolled past the green and into a sand trap. The putter would then be used for the fifth shot.

Each club in a matched set of golf clubs will have a number of common characteristics that must be suited to the individual player. These are:

The lie of the club.	The flex of the shaft.
The length of the club.	The swing weight of the club.
The thickness of the grip.	The loft of the clubhead.

THE LIE

The lie of the club is the angle that the leading edge of the clubhead takes in relation to the shaft of the club.

A shorter player will generally use a flatter-lying club, a taller golfer, a more upright one. When in a comfortable and correct stance (see page 16), the correct lie will result in the bottom, leading edge of the clubface being parallel to the ground. A tall player using a club meant for a shorter golfer will tend to send the ball veering off to the right (called a slice); when a short player uses a tall person's club, the ball will tend to veer left (a hook).

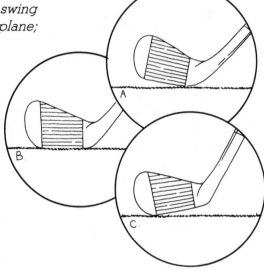

Figure 1: *The lie of the club: (A)—the swing plane is too wide; (B)—the correct swing plane; (C)—swing plane too steep.*

LENGTH

Generally speaking, there are only very slight variations in the length of a given club from set to set. Very little variation is necessary unless a golfer has a very unusual build. The lie of the club is usually enough to compensate for normal differences in build. A slightly longer club may help a shorter golfer get a little more distance on the fairway.

Figure 2: *The club length varies from the driver (far left) to the sand wedge.*

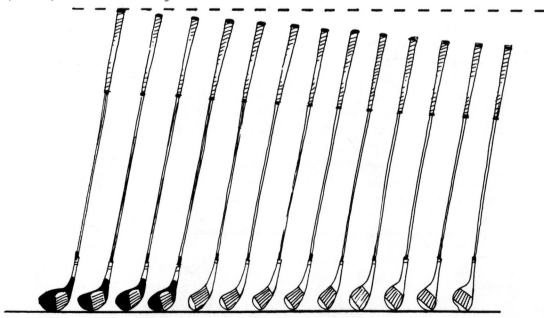

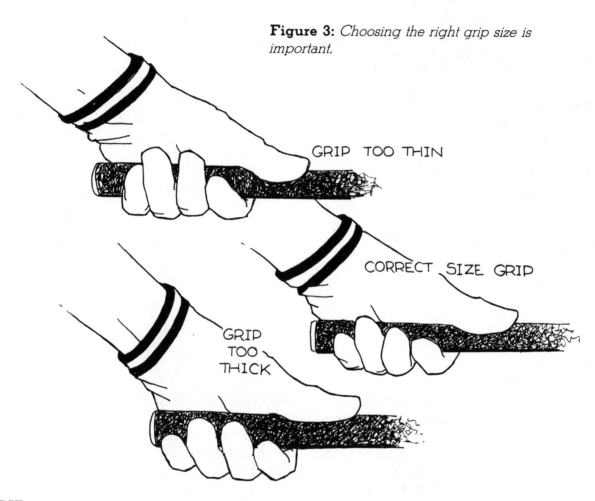

Figure 3: *Choosing the right grip size is important.*

GRIP TOO THIN

CORRECT SIZE GRIP

GRIP TOO THICK

GRIP

You must learn how to grip the club correctly in order to develop a good golf swing (see pages 12–14); in acquiring the correct grip, the thickness of the handle is a very important factor.

Grips come in thick, thin, and regular sizes: thicker for larger hands and thinner for smaller ones. They come in leather or rubber; rubber is recommended for ease of maintenance and economy.

Common advice would have hookers experiment on the driving range with thicker grips, slicers with thinner ones.

FLEX

Golf club shafts come in varying degrees of flexibility, or flex: XX, for extra-extra stiff; X, extra stiff; S, stiff; R, regular; A, less stiff; and L, ladies. The whippier L and A shafts provide more clubhead speed when hitting the ball, and so send the ball that little extra distance that a lightly muscled person may need. Unfortunately, the users of these shafts must sacrifice some control. The stiffer X and S shafts provide a good deal more control of the clubhead. They are more suited to a heavily muscled golfer who may not need extra distance but would like to keep the ball on the fairway. An R (regular) is about right for the average-build male weekend golfer.

Figure 4: *The flex of the shaft affects power and control.*

WEIGHT

The weight of each club is balanced so that the longer woods and irons (which are actually lighter) feel the same as the shorter, heavier clubs when they are swung. The clubs are weighted this way so that the golfer can maintain the all-important consistent swing. The clubhead can exceed 100 miles per hour when it is swung, so even fractional differences in weight can make a big difference. Swing weights are usually classified by letter: C weights are lighter and generally used by women; D weights are heavier and used by most men. D-1 is a good experimental starting weight for most male and female novice golfers.

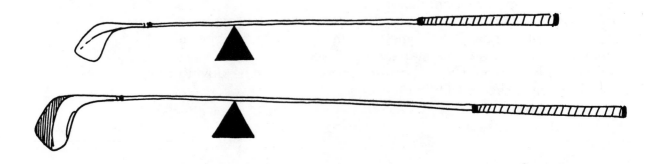

Figure 5: *Clubs in a set should be balanced to have a similar feel when swung.*

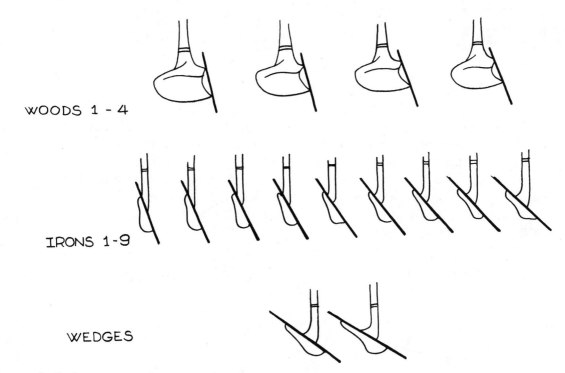

WOODS 1 - 4

IRONS 1-9

WEDGES

Figure 6: *Loft increases from woods to wedges. The most vertical lines represent the least loft.*

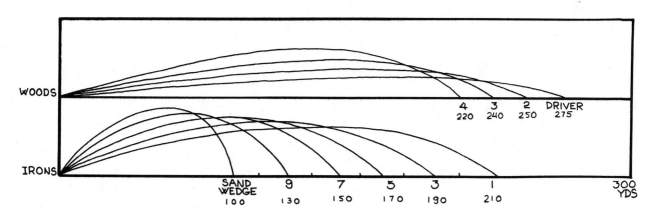

WOODS

4   3   2   DRIVER
220   240   250   275

IRONS

SAND WEDGE   9   7   5   3   1   300 YDS
100   130   150   170   190   210

Figure 7: *Ranges of the various clubs when swung by pros.*

LOFT

The amount of vertical tilt of a club is called its loft, and is illustrated in figure 6. Each kind of club has a specific standard loft. The loft determines the shape of the arc the ball will travel, and the amount of backspin the ball will have. The greater the angle of loft, the higher and shorter the arc of the ball in flight. Also, the greater the loft, the more backspin the ball will have and the sooner it should stop rolling after landing. Next to a consistent swing, understanding the capabilities of the various clubs is a golfer's main tool in controlling the ball.

9

Putters

The choice of putters is a matter of personal preference. It's very important to be both physically comfortable and confident with the putter you choose. For most golfers a putter with an upright lie and broad face helps in aiming. Most putters are weighted in the heel and toe and not centrally. Both proper weighting and central shafting tend to make a putter more forgiving of small errors, such as missing the putter head's "sweet spot" (or balance point). For comfort, choose a length of putter that matches your size and stance. Standard loft on a putter is 4 degrees.

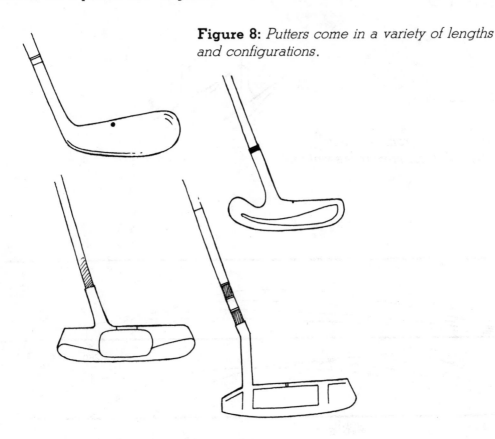

Figure 8: *Putters come in a variety of lengths and configurations.*

Club Maintenance

Keep your clubs dry, particularly if you have traditional woods, which may split or rot if stored damp. To help keep moisture out and protect them from scratches, make sure the varnish on woods is in good condition. Never let mud remain caked in the grooves or the face of your clubs. During play, for maximum control of spin on the next shot, take a rag or twig and scrape out any mud that may have become lodged in the head. Be careful not to damage the grips while removing or replacing clubs from an overfull bag. If you have leather grips, oil them frequently. Wash rubber ones occasionally with mild soapy water. When grips feel smooth and slippery, they are worn down and should be replaced.

Other Equipment

Here's a brief rundown of a few extra golfing necessities:

Good golf shoes with cleats offer firm support for your feet and calves, especially during your swing on a dewy morning when the grass is slippery. For a thirty-six-hole Saturday, you'll be glad you have them when walking all those miles.

A golf glove gives the feeling of maximum grip as the left hand swings the club. It is not absolutely necessary to wear one, although all but a few pros do. After all, sweaty hands are slippery hands. If you wear a golf glove on the driving range it will help prevent blisters, and if you practice with one you should play with one. Store the glove in a zip-lock plastic bag—don't let it dry out and crack.

Carts and bags are necessities. You don't want to mortgage your house to buy quality ones, but like many other purchases, really cheap carts and bags won't last. However, there are good buys to be found, so exercise some common sense. If you have only a few clubs, then a small "Sunday bag" will be all you'll need. Make sure the bag has a padded shoulder strap. But no matter how fine your equipment, never wheel carts or drag bags onto the greens.

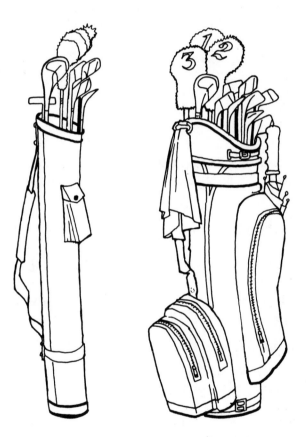

Figure 9: *A Sunday bag (left) is fine when you own only a few clubs. As you acquire more clubs, a roomier golf bag (right) is more appropriate.*

Balls are made with both solid and wound-rubber cores and both types come in various compressions ranging from 60 to 100. The higher the compression, the harder the ball and the farther it will fly; it will, however, be harder to control. A number of pros use a 100-compression ball, but it would be an exceptional weekender who did not get better results with a regular (90-compression) ball. At any rate, experiment, find a ball you feel comfortable with, and stick with it. More deeply dimpled balls can also be purchased that will help the golfer who has trouble getting the ball up—but these are no substitute for working on your swing.

3. Grip and Stance

Most golfers know that they must develop a consistent and fundamentally sound swing if they are to have any success with the sport. A related bit of knowledge that often fails to sink in is that a proper grip and stance before swinging the club will eliminate most of the problems that prevent a good swing. The seeds of most swing problems are planted in the grip and stance.

Grip

Just as the club is your only link to the ball, your grip is your only link to the club. If you grip the club correctly, your swing will have a very good chance of delivering the clubface to the ball at that instant that it is squared to the "target line" (see page 15).

Another advantage of a correct grip is that your hands will not allow the club to shift or slip at the backswing's highest point, or even upon impact with the ball. Also, your wrists will be able to hinge naturally and correctly during the swing.

The right and left hands have distinct functions in the golf grip, with the left hand providing a firm hold and the right hand controlling the movement and providing stability. (And vice versa for the left-hander; all instructions in this book should be reversed for left-handers.)

LEFT HAND

First align the clubhead behind the ball, aiming at your target. The clubhead should be resting on a line that could be drawn straight back along the clubhead and pass an inch or so to the right of your left heel, as shown in figure 15, line D. Your left hand should reach out naturally to grasp the club so that your arm is relatively straight (but comfortable, not ramrod stiff). Your straight left arm should line up with the club shaft. Now turn your hand downward so that the handle of the club touches both the palm and the fingers, as shown in figure 10. Close your hand around the club so that your thumb is pointing nearly straight down and just slightly to the right. Your grip should be firm enough that you feel a secure hold on the club but not so strong that it causes your forearm to feel tight.

If you were to lift the club vertically in front of you, you should feel pressure on the pad of your hand.

RIGHT HAND

Now, while continuing to grasp the club in your left hand, let the handle of the club lie diagonally across the base of the fingers of your right hand (see figure 11). Close your hand around the club so that the thumb points down the shaft and slightly to the left; you should be aware of controlling the club with your fingers rather than the heel pad, as in your left hand.

Figure 10: *Proper positioning of the left hand.*

Figure 11: *Proper positioning of the right hand.*

BOTH HANDS

Raise the pinky finger of your right hand and slide your right hand up the handle until you can overlap the space between the first and second fingers on your left hand with the right pinky. Once you have achieved what seems to be a satisfactory grip, it should feel as if both hands are functioning as a single unit. The left and right palms should be facing each other at right angles to the clubface. This will greatly increase your chance of delivering the clubface square to the ball at the moment of impact.

A golfer who is grasping the club too tightly will tend to hook the ball. Tension in your grip is contagious. It will stiffen your entire body and ruin your swing.

A golfer whose grip is not firm enough will tend to slice.

Figure 13: *The hands should be perpendicular to the target.*

Figure 12: *A good grip.*

Figure 14: *The Vardon grip (A); the interlocking grip (B); and the full-fingered grip (C).*

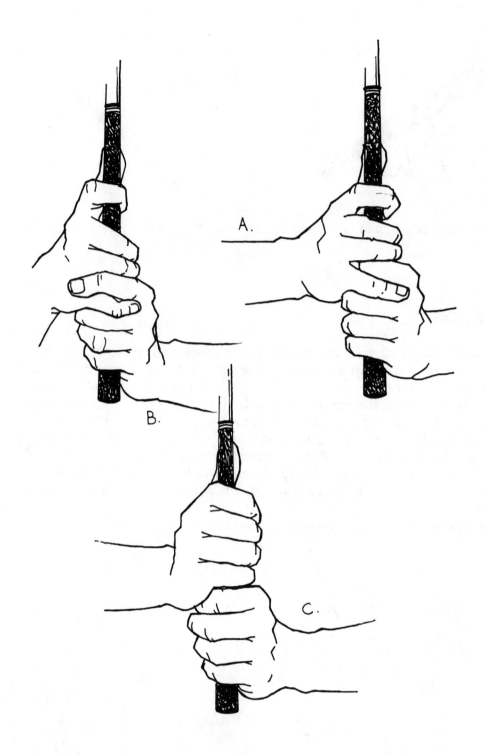

The grip described above is known as the overlapping grip, as shown in (A) of figure 14. It was developed by Harry Vardon nearly a century ago. It has stood the test of time and is used by more golfers than any other. There are two other popular grips, also illustrated in figure 14: the interlocking grip (B) and the full-fingered grip (C). They are very much worth experimenting with during practice to see which one is best suited to your hands.

Aiming

For the ball to travel in the intended direction, the clubface should be at a right angle to the target line—the line on which you want the ball to fly. First, when aiming, visualize a line through your ball and to the target, let's say the flag at the green on the sixth hole of Augusta National, as shown in (A) of figure 15. It helps to pick out a reference point along that line, just a few feet in front of the ball: a sprig or a dead leaf will do nicely (B).

Now put the club just behind the ball so that the lower leading edge of the clubhead is at a 90-degree angle to the target line that you imagined. Allow the grip of the club to point up into your left hip.

Take a stance (more on stance later, right now we're just aiming) with your feet shoulder-width apart, your left foot slightly ahead of the ball. Both feet are perpendicular to a new imaginary line parallel to your target line, but a few feet to the side of it, as shown in (C) of figure 15.

Skillful golf is about accuracy. You should take great care when aligning your club. Always align your club first and then adjust your stance to work with that alignment (D). If you do it the other way around, the temptation to adjust the clubhead without also adjusting your stance will be very great. Failure to do both will throw off your aim.

As golfers master the game, they learn to assume more open stances (slightly facing the target) or closed stances (slightly turned away from it). They also begin to contact the ball with an intentionally open or closed clubface. A clubface angled slightly back to the right is called "open"; one that is turned slightly forward to the left is called "closed." They do this in order to use spin to control the trajectory of the ball. Knowledge of the physics of these kinds of shots can also be a very helpful diagnostic tool when hooking or slicing. Golfers, however, should begin by striving to aim the ball with a squared clubface, its sole resting on the ground while the golfer is in a squared stance.

Figure 15: *The target line (A); reference point (B); parallel stance (C); and clubhead alignment (D).*

Stance

Your stance when addressing the ball, just like your grip, should be comfortable and natural. If you take up an awkward stance when addressing the ball, you will certainly not be able to swing the golf club comfortably and correctly.

Depending on the club you are using, your feet will be more or less shoulder-width apart. The woods and long irons require a wider stance, while the shorter irons require a progressively narrower stance. Rest your weight equally on both toes and heels; the shorter the iron you are using, the slightly more weight you need to put on your front leg, the leg nearer the target. When teeing off or driving from the fairway, turn your left foot slightly outward in the direction of the target and distribute your weight equally between both feet. Align the tips of your feet parallel to the intended line of flight.

You should be in a generally upright and comfortable, balanced position, knees slightly bent, and bending slightly at the waist toward the ball.

Figure 16: *Side view of a good relaxed stance.*

Figure 17: *Front view of a good relaxed stance.*

Ball Placement

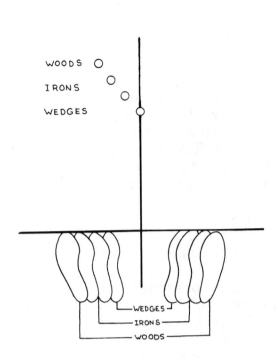

Figure 18: *The older, alternate system.*

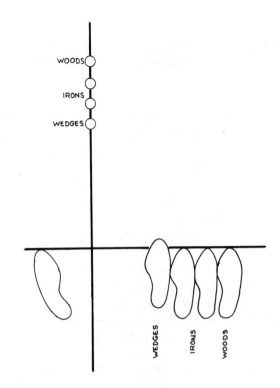

Figure 19: *The stationary-left-foot system of stance alignment.*

There are two schools of thought about where to take up the stance in relation to the ball. One way of thinking has you shift your entire position depending on the club used (figure 18); the other places the left foot in a relatively stationary position in relation to the ball, no matter what club you are using. While both are viable systems, the stationary-left-foot system is the more modern of the two, and it has the advantage of allowing you to swing in basically the same way no matter which club you are using. This is helpful in promoting consistency.

Again, as illustrated in figure 15, take up your stance so that the imaginary line that is drawn through the ball and perpendicular to the line of flight will pass an inch to the right of your left heel. There can be no set rule about the exact distance to stand from the ball. It depends on your height, club length, the arc of your swing, and what you find comfortable. Obviously, you will take your stance farther away with a long driver than you would with a short 9-iron.

While always leaving your left foot stationary, your right foot will be moved farther back and your weight will be more evenly distributed between the two when using the longer clubs (figure 19). You will take a narrower stance with shorter clubs, moving your right foot closer to and putting your weight slightly more on the left foot.

When addressing the ball, develop a routine of steps that you *always* follow. It will help build consistency and be of great help in improving your concentration. Make a habit of starting the ritual with visualization before you address the ball. Don't just "think positive," but visualize your best shot in great detail—from the swing and the ball's flight to the moment when the ball lands on the grass.

4. The Swing

The Golf Swing

All aspects of the perfect golf swing have been analyzed in minute detail, from every angle and from every philosophical perspective. Fortunately, the experts agree on two important points. One: any golfer can learn the golf swing and do well with it if he or she is willing to practice. Two: that same golfer must be capable of being reasonably analytical and at the same time relaxed enough to go ahead and swing the club without being paralyzed by analysis.

Until now, the elements of golf we've looked at have been the elements that you can easily control. Club selection, grip, aim, and stance are all vitally important aspects of the game, but they are all aspects that you can pretty easily prepare and control.

Now we're going to try to put these controllable preparations together and into motion. The whole process starts slowly, but before long the clubhead is moving faster than 100 miles per hour. At that speed, an error of a quarter-inch can make the difference between a score of par or a double-bogey. This is why it is so enormously helpful to have someone observing you, optimally the club pro.

Again, remember the experts agree that the swing *can be learned* through *practice.* While no two golfers' swings are exactly alike, all *good* golf swings are based on understanding and adhering to a few vital principles. Foremost is that you are not trying to *hit the ball,* you are trying to *swing* the club *properly.*

So let's get the club moving. We'll start, like the stroke does, with the backswing.

The Backswing

The backswing begins the stroke; it should not actually be a ''swing'' at all but a gradual cocking of the wrists, the arms, shoulders, hips, and legs. A proper backswing sets the stage for a good swing. Because the two are so interrelated, before we look at the backswing, we should understand a few ideas about the golf swing in general:

SPEED

- The greater the speed the clubhead is traveling when it strikes the ball, the greater distance the ball will fly. You *cannot* muscle the club and force distance, you *must* let the club swing and therefore let centrifugal force do the job.

SWING PLANE

- The great golfer Ben Hogan has been credited with first popularizing the concept of the swing plane. When the golf club is swung properly, the club, hands, and left arm travel in a circular arc tilted at an angle around the body, as shown in figure 20. Its hub, which should remain fixed, is located at the base of the neck, where the shoulders meet.
- The wrists must cock during the backswing and release during the swing. This is the only way that clubhead speed can be achieved. They should cock and uncock in the same plane as the rest of the swing.
- The angular momentum of the club and arms will naturally bring the clubhead to the ball without extra muscular effort from the hands or arms.
- A steady head is absolutely essential if a golfer is to swing accurately through the ball.

Figure 20: *The swing plane.*

WAGGLE AND TRIGGER MOVEMENT

- After setting up, you will want to waggle the club, making a few short backward-and-forward practice motions with your club. It will help you visualize your swing plane. It also helps to ensure that your hands and wrists, which might tighten up at this point, remain supple.
- A slight forward bending of the right knee toward the target accompanied by a very slight pressing forward with the hands makes a good unobtrusive motion with which to trigger the backswing.
- The waggle and trigger movements should be performed as a ritual before every shot.

Now we'll return specifically to the backswing. It is important to remember that the backswing both establishes the swing plane and creates a rhythm that will affect the quality of the swing.

Figures 21 through 23 illustrate the step-by-step movements of the backswing. The hands and arms begin moving first, followed immediately by the shoulders, with the left shoulder beginning to turn under the chin. As you move the club away from the ball, watch it to make sure that it remains square to the ball for a short distance before it begins the upward motion.

The left wrist begins to cock so that the club, which began in line with the left arm, begins to turn back until it is at the top of the backswing. While remaining within the swing plane, the club is now angled at least 90 degrees to the left arm.

Meanwhile, as the left wrist bends, so does the right wrist, hinging back as the right elbow points downward.

The large muscles of the body must be allowed into action. The hips will naturally follow the shoulders in a coiling turn of the body. The left knee will begin to bend automatically, while the left heel raises slightly. Your weight will shift back onto your straighter (but not stiff) right leg. This will help maintain the level of the shoulders and the swing plane.

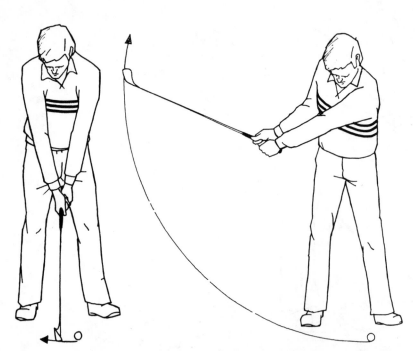

Figure 21: *The takeaway.*   **Figure 22:** *The backswing.*   **Figure 23:** *Fully cocked and ready to swing. Notice foot positioning.*

At the top of the coiled backswing, the club shaft will ideally be horizontal to the ground and also parallel to the target line. The shoulders will be turned back at least 90 degrees from where they began when you addressed the ball. The hip will be angled at about 45 degrees. The head must be kept still during the backswing, as it should during the swing that follows. But after all, we're talking about a human body, not a fence post. The head will naturally turn slightly to the right as the rest of the body does. If you allow it to do so only slightly, while keeping a steady left eye on the ball, this will actually help the swing. But remember, if you lose control and begin to move your head rather than just swiveling it slightly, your foundation for a good swing is destroyed.

Elements of a Good Swing

Swinging the club correctly is a function of reflex, relaxation, and confidence. Its success also depends on careful preparation in the stance and backswing and *on lots of practice on the driving range.*

Footwork is the basis of a good swing and if you can manage to keep your body moving in a natural, coordinated way, the rest of the swing should be easy.

First, to start the swing, return your left heel, which was raised during the backswing, solidly to the ground while driving your weight off your right leg. As you swing, you will be transferring your weight to the left by sliding your hips back square with the ball, the way they were at address. As the swing progresses, the natural rotation of your hips will continue along with the shift of your weight to your forward, left foot.

As your swing progresses you will have transferred your weight from the inside of your right foot to the inside of your left foot and then finally to the outside of your left foot. Your right knee will end up pointing in the direction

Figure 24: *The swing begins; the left heel drops.*

Figure 25: *As the swing progresses, the hips turn.*

of flight and your right heel will be lifted well off the ground. For practice, concentrate on the footwork and hip rotation without even trying to hit a ball or swing a club. As you go through the pantomime motions, just swing your extended arms, keeping them in the swing plane. Remember to keep your head still.

It is important to have a mental picture of the club, returning in a wide arc to the ball, as it follows the swing plane you defined during the takeaway and backswing. In reality, it will probably return to the ball very slightly inside that plane, but it will do this of its own accord and is not in any way a problem.

After you begin to transfer your weight to the left side during the swing, you pull the club downward with your straight left arm, as if pulling a bell rope, allowing your wrists to uncock and your left arm and the club to swing through the ball. The swing should never be a pushing action with the right arm but rather a pulling action with your left. Remember that although you should not consciously push or swing the club with your right hand, neither should your right hand and arm restrain the club from swinging. If you want a delayed and more powerful swing of the club, simply let the hands follow the arms, which follow the shoulders, and so on.

All the actions of the feet, then hips, then trunk, then shoulders, then arms, then hands should flow together, *allowing* the clubhead to swing, allowing it to reach its greatest possible speed at the moment it strikes the ball, and allowing your whole, uncoiling body and your technique to supply the power.

Remember, the upper body and club will usually do the right things naturally, provided that your legs and lower body move correctly and you don't try too hard to *hit* the ball with your hands and arms.

If you have assumed the correct stance and executed a well-coordinated backswing, your body mechanics, in the form of energy released through the club, should line the clubhead up at the right angle to the target line. This will happen without any conscious manipulation of the club with your hands.

Figure 26: *At the bottom of the swing, the wrists automatically begin to uncock as the right knee flexes.*

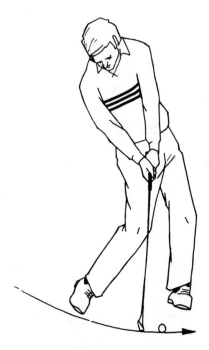

Figure 27: *Striking the ball: left arm straight and head down.*

Many golfers benefit from imagining the clubhead is an Olympic-style hammer on the end of a long cable. When swinging the club, they imagine the club shaft is the cable and the head the hammer, and then they swing accordingly. Give this image a try—it might work for you.

Follow-through

Logically, the follow-through should have nothing to do with the flight of a ball. After all, the ball has already left the clubhead and is probably 35 or 40 yards down the fairway. So who cares about follow-through? You should, because mentally it has everything to do with making a good shot. Visualizing the details of a good follow-through before each swing and trying to act on that visualization can help you keep your head down during impact, and not jerk it up ahead of time, affecting your swing.

It is also helpful to imagine a nice high straight follow-through moving momentarily along the target line before it follows the swing plane. This may not be an accurate visualization of what the clubhead does, but putting that image into action could very well help your accuracy. Similarly, by trying to keep the shoulders and club in line with the swing plane even on the follow-through, a much more consistent stroke can result.

As you become familiar with your own swinging pattern, your follow-through can become an excellent diagnostic tool to help make the constant, minor adjustments to your swing that most golfers find necessary. On the full swing, the body should end facing the target with the club behind the head.

Figure 28: *Avoid the temptation to lift your head too early in the follow-through.*

Figure 29: *Nice relaxed follow-through.*

5. Down the Fairway

Let's look at how the basic swing technique applies to the various woods, irons, and wedges that get you where you want to be—on the green and near the cup.

Tee Shot

What you want out of a tee shot is to get down the fairway. It is important for any golfer to strike a balance between distance and accuracy and do it with an eye for tactics. Sometimes a 250-yard drive into the rough on a par 5 will do you a whole lot more good than a 175-yard shot to the middle of the fairway; other times the reverse is true.

Tee up the ball so that the top half of the ball lines up above the clubhead at address. Although you will have to work out the exact position through trial and error, make sure to position the ball so that it is more or less aligned with your left heel. The idea is that the ball should be hit at the bottom of your swing—*or even a little on the upswing.* So take as wide a stance as you find comfortable; for most people, feet about shoulder-width apart is just right.

Figure 30: *Proper height of the ball when teeing up.*

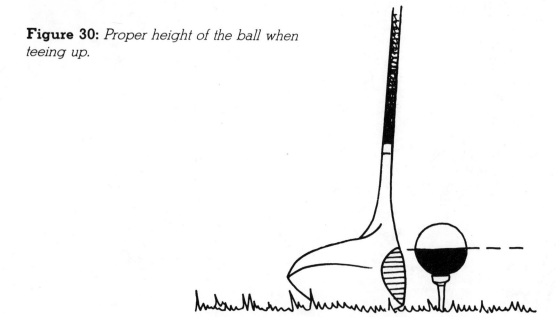

Fairway Woods

Take a slightly narrower stance, so that rather than hitting on the upswing, you are making contact with the golf ball at the bottom of your swing. These clubs are more lofted than the driver, so avoid the temptation to hit the ball on the upswing as you did on the tee shot. The loft will lift the ball by itself.

Remember, the ball is not on a tee now, and if you're not careful, you'll end up topping the ball, that is, sending it skimming along the ground.

Irons

The irons are your best buddies, offering you the greatest number of options to shape the flight of the ball. The long irons—1,2,3—should be played more like the woods. The novice might want to begin with the 3-iron rather than the 1. In fact, the shorter irons are the ones beginning golfers most easily learn to trust. To use them, you must take a still-narrower stance so that you "hit down on the ball." Allow the loft of the club to get the ball up in the air; this will result in your taking a divot (a lump of turf) in front of the ball after you sweep through it with the stroke.

It should be becoming obvious that each club will require you to adjust your stance. The longer clubs—driver, woods, and long irons—require you to take a wider stance with your feet. The shorter clubs, such as the 7-, 8-, and 9-irons, and pitching wedges, require a narrower stance.

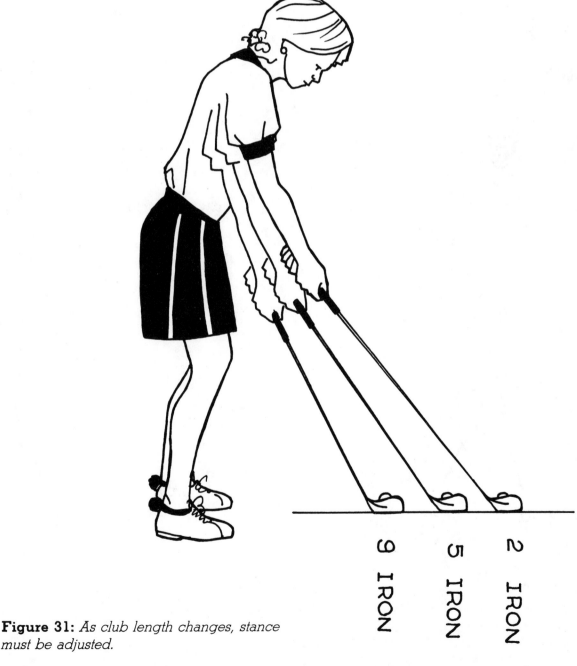

9 IRON   5 IRON   2 IRON

Figure 31: *As club length changes, stance must be adjusted.*

The wider base helps you keep your balance when swinging the longer clubs and allows you to turn your hips more for greater power. The narrower stance allows you to rest more weight on your left (forward) leg, which helps you control the swing and lets the clubhead do its job. Not only will the stance be narrower for the shorter clubs, but the shorter clubs also require a shorter backswing and less of a hip turn. The shorter the backswing, the shorter the follow-through; a three-quarter backswing taken with a 7-iron should end in a three-quarter follow-through; a three-eighths swing with a pitching wedge should end in a three-eighths follow-through. (See figures 32 and 33.)

Figure 32: *The three-quarters backswing will be mirrored by the three-quarters follow-through.*

Figure 33: *Three-quarters follow-through.*

Getting Closer to the Green

As you work your way up to the higher-numbered clubs and your stance becomes narrower, you'll notice how much less weight you transfer from back to front, that is, right to left leg. The transfer happens much more quickly than the gradual turning transition you make in your wider stances. Despite all these superficial (but important) changes, the swing should remain the same comfortable, repeatable, basic swing from tee to green. You've polished it on the practice range and it got you this far, so if your tee shot at the third hole ends up in the trees, don't start fiddling with your basic grip, stance, or backswing. That's work you do on the practice range.

Remember, it is almost inevitable that some of your long-iron shots will skim along the ground after you've topped them. When this happens, just make up your mind to concentrate next time on shifting your weight from right to left. Also decide to trust the club to get the ball up with its loft and remember that, paradoxically, you must hit slightly down; it will feel as if you are pinching the ball between club and earth to get the ball up. Avoid the temptation to lift the club, scooping at the ball with your wrists. The result of this error will be a follow-through that ends with your weight on your back (right) leg and a worse topping than you had before. And as ever, keep your head down and your eye on the ball.

When you find yourself too near the green to take a full swing but not near enough to putt, you have two options: a high lofted shot that drops with backspin onto the green, called a pitch shot and illustrated by line A in figure 34; or a chip shot, a sort of long putt that starts with a shallow hop over an obstacle or rough that is preventing you from putting accurately, as demonstrated by line B in figure 34.

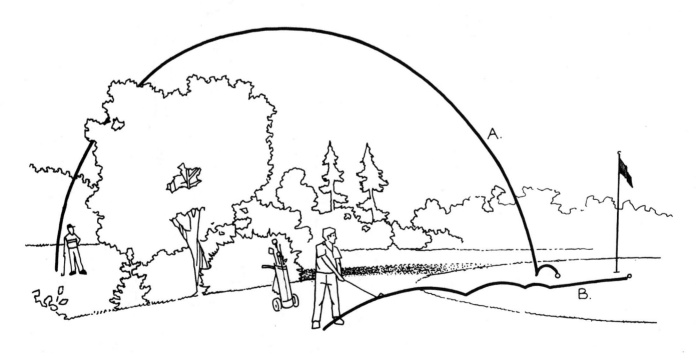

Figure 34: *A pitch shot (A) and a chip-and-run (B).*

The pitch shot is generally hit with a 9-iron, pitching wedge, or sand wedge.

For the pitch, you should open your stance a little more so you are turned slightly toward the target; also, open the clubface slightly to compensate for the adjusted stance. The angled clubface will also give you more loft and spin. A pitch shot uses an abbreviated version of the normal swing. The backswing (see figure 35) and follow-through (see figure 36) should be shortened in proportion to the distance you need. Swing slowly and deliberately, but nevertheless *swing* and get some clubhead speed. Since it's an iron, swing down on the ball as you would with any iron and let the clubface do the work.

Figure 35: *A pitch shot. Plenty of wrist movement.*

Figure 36: *Swinging normally and avoiding the temptation to scoop.*

Avoiding the natural temptation to scoop the ball with your wrists is very important. It will help if you adjust your stance so that the greater part of your weight is on your left foot and shifts only slightly during the backswing. When addressing the ball, make sure that your left arm is straight and your hands are slightly ahead of the ball; the club shaft is no longer perpendicular to the target line but angled slightly.

When your ball is separated from the green by a good deal of rough, making it impossible to putt, a chip-and-run shot is what you'll need. Think of it as a long putt with a little hop at the outset to help you get over the danger. You will usually use a 5- or 6-iron, clubs which have just enough loft to send the ball over the tall grass and roll the ball onto the green. When you grip the club for this shot, choke way down on the handle until your arms hang nearly vertically. Make sure that your straight left arm and hands are well ahead of the ball; rest your weight primarily on your left foot and don't attempt to lift the ball with your wrists. Even though you swing the club more like a putter, with a squared clubface and little wrist action, it's important to remember to hit slightly *down* on the ball, sweeping through like you would with any other iron. Positioning for the shot is illustrated in figures 37 and 38. Again, let the clubhead do the work.

With both the pitch and the chip-and-run it is most important to remember to set up a nice slow rhythm within the backswing, but to accelerate through the ball with enough speed to give you the control you need.

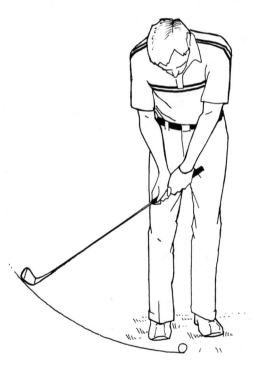

Figure 37: *Choking up on the club for the chip shot.*

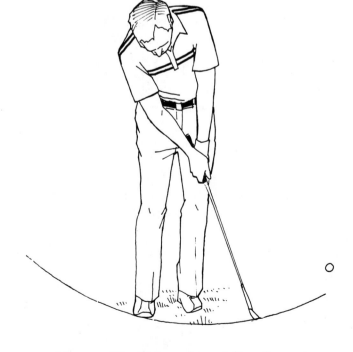

Figure 38: *Chip-and-run follow-through.*

6. Trouble

In real life, a perfect tee shot that drops to a perfect lie in the middle of the fairway happens, at best, to some of the people some of the time. Few of these occasions feature a novice golfer.

It's easy to become unsettled when a difficult lie presents itself. But a calm, experienced golfer plans his or her strategy for escape in a rational way, with an eye toward the overall score, and not just the present predicament.

Some of the challenges to a golfer's serenity during a round include a steep uphill or downhill lie, sand traps, deep rough, woods, water hazards, wind, and occasionally, rain. Since these challenges often seem to come in pairs, this is where experience and creativity pay off.

Sloping Ground

When the ball comes to rest on oddly angled ground, remember to maintain your balance, thereby minimizing the effect the height difference between your feet and the ball has on your swing.

UPHILL LIE

In your stance, lean to your right (downhill) so that you are somewhat more perpendicular to the hillside, as shown in figure 39. This will have the effect of giving you a flat lie. (Resist the tendency to lean to the left.) You can easily balance yourself this way; however, there is little room to swing the club. To help keep your balance while leaning downhill, use more arm and less body in your swing. The angle at which you are leaning on the slope will cause the ball to sail more steeply upward than if you were standing flat, so use a less lofted club than the one you would normally choose.

Figure 39: *Adjusting for an uphill lie.*

DOWNHILL LIE

The same principle applies for a downhill lie as for an uphill one: get your body perpendicular to the slope and maintain your balance. Rest most of your weight on your left (downhill) leg. Since the slope and swing will naturally shoot the ball downward, use a more lofted club than you normally would. (See figure 40.)

Figure 40: *Adjusting for a downhill lie.*

BALL ABOVE YOUR FEET

Again, establish a balanced stance perpendicular to the hillside. The ball will tend to fly to the left, so open your clubface slightly. Choke up on the club to make sure that you don't take a major divot. (Figure 41 illustrates the principle of this shot.) Since this will affect your distance, choose your club accordingly.

Figure 41: *Adjusting for a ball above the feet.*

BALL BELOW YOUR FEET

If you choke up on the club for a ball *above* your feet, it makes sense that you would grip the club at the very end to reach a ball below them, right? No. What you do in this situation is bend more than usual at the knees and remind yourself to keep a steady head during the swing; close the clubface slightly, and swing deliberately so that you can maintain your balance.

Figure 42: *Adjusting for a ball below the feet.*

Sand Traps

After landing in the bunker, the golfer's first thought is, "Please, let me out of here, and fast." This prayer will only be answered if the golfer makes getting out the first priority. It should take precedence over any desire to redeem yourself or to minimize the disappointment and embarrassment of the failed shot with a spectacular next one.

Since each sand trap situation is different, bunker play demands calmness, concentration, analysis, and a steady controlled swing to free you from the trap.

Figure 43: *A splash shot.*

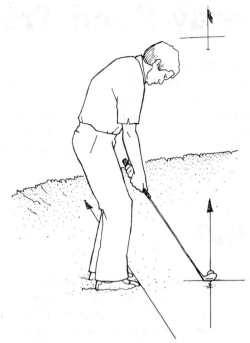

Figure 44: *Feet worked in and clubface open; do not ground club.*

Figure 45: *Aiming with an open stance.*

The trick to escaping a sand trap near the green is *not* to lob the ball out but to lob out the *sand* in which the ball is embedded. The ball will come out with it. Use the sand wedge to execute this "splash shot." First, work your feet into the sand until you have a solid foundation and a good feel for the consistency of the sand. This will also be the only legal way to test the sand, since you are not ever allowed to touch your club to the sand, or "ground" your club, in a trap before the shot. When addressing the ball, your stance should be open (turned slightly to the left) and your clubface open (turned slightly to the right, but square with the target). Swing just as if you were hitting a pitch shot but twice as hard for the distance you want the ball to cover. Cut the club into the sand an inch or so behind the ball. A good deal of sand, and the ball, will be splashed out of the bunker. Concentrate on turning your right hand under the left and raising the clubhead (and not your head to see how you did) on the follow-through.

If your ball is deeply impacted in the sand, you will have to swing harder, blasting it out with an accelerating stroke that arcs considerably under the ball and takes a lot of beachfront out of the bunker with it. This ball will have very little backspin so it will roll a good deal.

Figure 46: *Cutting under the ball.*

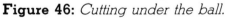
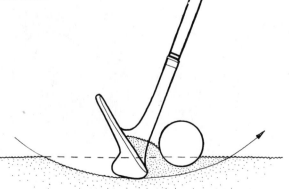

Fairway Sand Traps

Often your ball will roll gently to a stop in a fairway sand trap. You'll still have a lot of ground to cover with your next shot, so unless you are near the steep front lip or embedded in sand (and so forced to play a splash shot), you should treat this as a normal lie and take a normal swing, making as little contact with the sand as possible. Use a lofted club so you will feel sure of getting the ball over the lip; this helps you swing easily and naturally.

Rough

Like a ball in the sand trap, a ball lying in deep rough is no cause for alarm. The choice of a highly lofted club minimizes in two ways the entangling effect of the rough. First, entanglement of the club is lessened by the shorter shaft, which keeps the swing plane more upright and helps the club slip through the vegetation. Second, the lofted club will help to lift the ball out quickly before it becomes entangled again by the hay. A nice steep swing should help you minimize the amount of vegetation you trap between the club and the ball at impact. A firm grip will help to keep the clubface from twisting out of alignment as it slips through.

If the rough is particularly heavy, consider using a sand wedge, which has a heavier head than other irons.

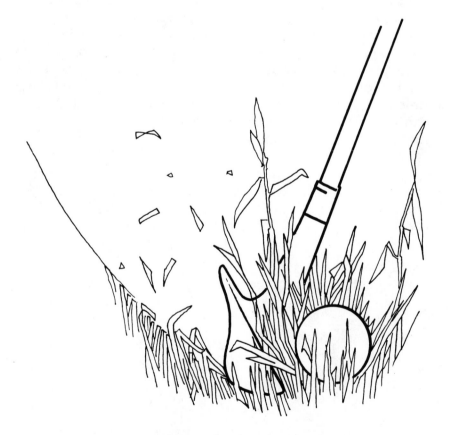

Figure 47: *A steep swing plane and a highly lofted club help to avoid entanglement.*

Trees and Bushes

Although some people will tell you that trees are 90 percent air, try shooting 100 golf balls at one and see what happens. You'll be lucky if ten come down on the other side. Go over, under, or around trees and bushes—ignore the temptation to go through them.

Water Hazards

Unless the ball is at least halfway out of the water and not embedded in muck, take a one-stroke penalty and drop the ball. If you attempt to hit a ball that is more than half-submerged, all you'll get is a pair of wet feet, a wasted stroke added to your score, and a one-stroke penalty when you do come to your senses and abandon the attempt and drop the ball.

Figure 48: *It's usually wiser to accept the one-stroke penalty and drop out of a water hazard.*

Wind and Rain

The first rule for playing on windy or rainy days is: no complaining. Everyone playing with you is affected by the weather, so you're all laboring under the same handicap. You may not fare well in these conditions, but then again, you may come out on top.

Golfers should take note of the direction and strength of the wind. What seems like a gentle breeze to us under the shelter of the trees can prove to be a 20-knot wind tossing through the treetops. Remember, that's the height at which the ball will be traveling. Use this knowledge to your advantage, as in figure 49. Getting the ball up with accuracy is always the key to success in the rain, so avoid the use of flat-faced clubs. The good news is that the ball will stop more readily on a soggy green so you can take some chances there. Two general rules of thumb: on an unpredictable windy day keep the ball down and on a wet day get it up; similarly, when the breeze is against you, keep the ball low; when the breeze is with you, get the ball up.

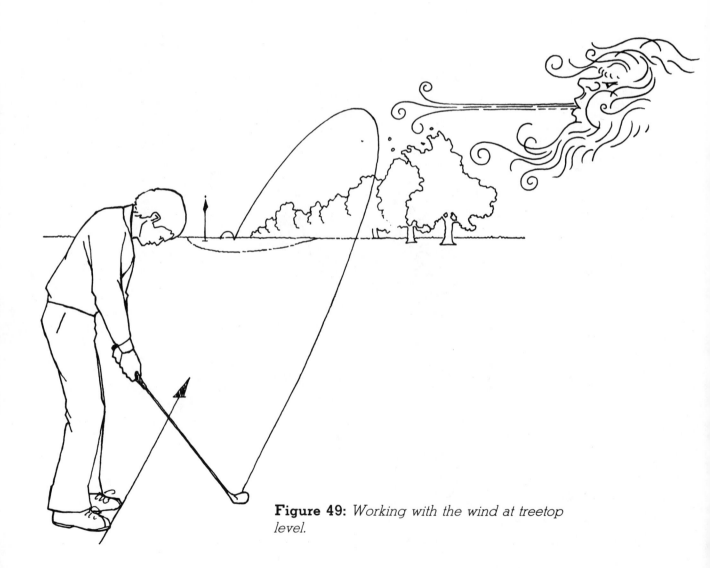

Figure 49: *Working with the wind at treetop level.*

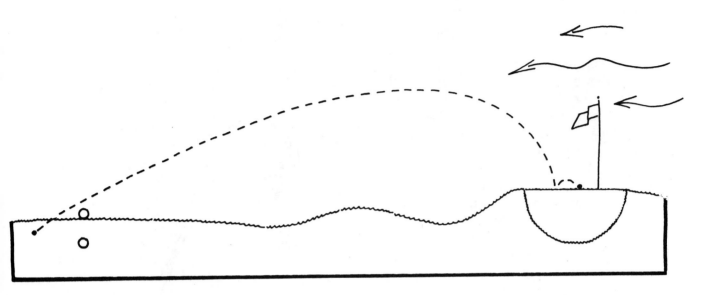

Figure 50: *Driving low into the wind.*

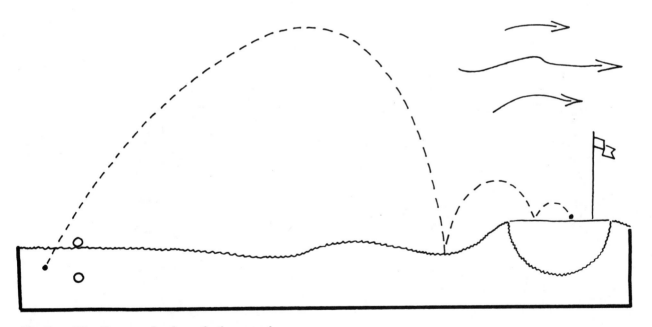

Figure 51: *Driving high with the wind.*

Unplayable Lie

With any "unplayable" ball, first weigh
your chances for success against the
one-stroke unplayable-lie penalty. If
you are unable to take your normal
stance to the left of the ball because
the ball is resting against a tree trunk,
for example, one option is to approach
the ball from the right rather than from
the left. Choose a club with a large
face, turn the club over, and reverse
your grip, with your left hand below
your right one. (See figure 53.) This
will mean that you are still coming at
the ball with the face of the club.
Swing as smoothly as you can.

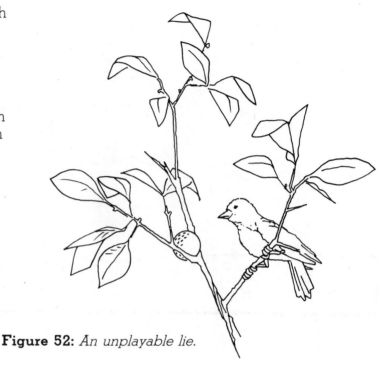

Figure 52: *An unplayable lie.*

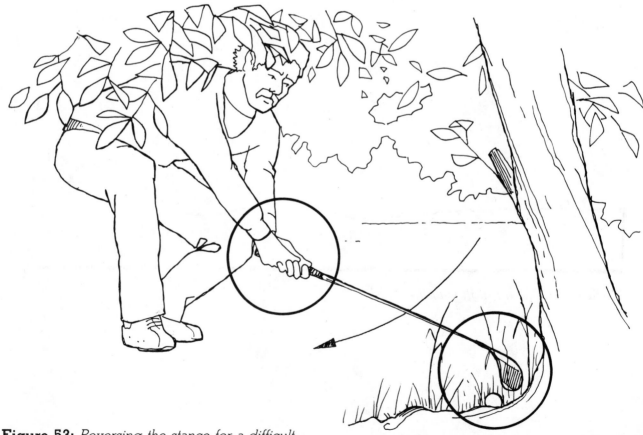

Figure 53: *Reversing the stance for a difficult
shot.*

7. Putting

Some say that there are two games being played on the golf course. One is golf, which has everything to do with getting the ball in the air; the other game is putting, which is all about rolling the ball along the ground.

If you can learn to putt you can play golf with anyone—or almost anyone. At any rate, the putter is your most frequently used club. When you start consistently breaking 100, then you'll find that on average during an eighteen-hole game of golf, you'll use your woods twenty or so times, your irons about forty times, and your putter, forty. It is important to note that one club, your putter, is used for *40 percent* of the shots. Obviously, once you are using your putter respectably most of the time, it's going to have a big impact on your overall game. Remember, more often than not the pros earn their birdies with their putters, so why not start shaving strokes off your game right away?

While it is true that successful putting depends greatly on a feel for the distance to the cup and an ability to read the slope and texture of the green, most good putters also employ a few common putting principles. It would be a mistake not to strike a balance between these principles and your intuitive skills.

Figure 54: *A feel for distance is the most essential element in putting.*

The Putter

That the choice of putter is a very personal matter is borne out by the huge variety of putters offered on the market. In learning to develop consistent putting, choose a standard-length (34 or 35 inches), balanced-feeling, heel- and toe-weighted putter. Choose one with a long blade, which you'll find easier to aim, and a shaft that enters the blade near the center, which will reduce twisting on off-center hits. A putter has a very slight loft, normally 4 degrees.

As your putting game develops, it's fun to experiment with different putters, since not only will confidence in your putter breathe confidence into your game, but it will encourage you to work on the practice green as well.

On the Green

The accomplished putter has consciously worked to develop the ability to read the green. It is much more common to find sloped or undulating greens than flat ones, but often the slope is so subtle that it is hard to perceive. It is a common error to strike too hard when the hole is downhill; when the hole is uphill, the ball is often struck too softly. If the green slopes across the line of the putt, then you must do what is called "playing the break" of the putt; that is, aiming for an imaginary target above the cup and allowing gravity to force the ball down the slope and into the hole. Begin to judge the slope of the green as you are walking up to it from the fairway.

When you get there, another way to judge how to play the break is to use the putter as a plumb bob, as illustrated in figures 55 and 56. First, squat a good distance from the ball and look through the ball at right angles to the line of the slope. Allow the putter to hang between your thumb and forefinger, visually lining up the ball and the shaft (see figure 56). Make sure the blade is lined up also, so its weight won't tilt the putter askew. If you now draw in your mind's eye a horizontal line from the cup through your shaft, the point where they cross will be your aiming point. This is a helpful aid, but not a foolproof system. Much depends on the speed and texture of the green and on your putting touch.

Another common aiming problem is that the green will present you with a compound slope over which to putt. Allow more for the break when putting a compound downhill angle, allow less for it when putting on a compound uphill slope. If you are unsure, play it safe and aim a little high. Your number-one asset, a feel for distance, becomes proportionately more important with the length of the putt. Even the direction the grass is lying can affect the tail end of a long putt. On the long ones, take some pressure off yourself by imagining that the hole is 3 feet in diameter and just aim for that. Your goal is to two-putt—to get close enough on your first try to be sure to sink the second shot. If you can two-putt most of the long ones, and if you happen to birdie a few in one putt, then you're doing great!

Figure 55: *Sloping greens require special aiming techniques.*

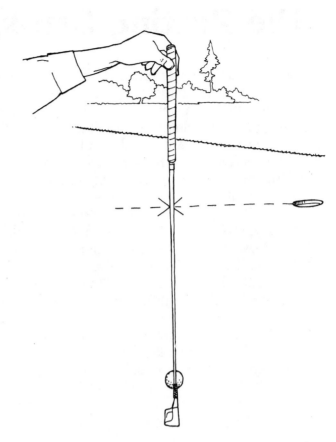

Figure 56: *Aim using the plum bob method.*

Figure 57: *Compound slopes and ball speed affect the curve of the trajectory.*

The Putting Stroke

After assessing the green and estimating how to play the break, you must do only two simple things: One, stroke the face of the putter through the ball square with the target line; and two, hit the ball just firmly enough to get it to the cup—two simple things that cause golfers to tear out their hair.

It is very important that the golfer remember to keep everything square to the target line—feet, hips, shoulders, arms, palms, and the face of the putter.

Grip the putter slightly down on the handle, so your palms face each other straight up and down the handle. (See figure 58.) To do so, first grip the handle in your left hand. The right hand then takes its grip facing and below the left hand. The right thumb should also point straight down the shaft. Now, lift your left forefinger and slide your right hand up into the gap left by it. Then, close your raised left forefinger back over the fingers of your right hand. This is known as the reverse overlapping grip and is illustrated in figure 59. Although it is very common, it is not the only successful putting grip used, by any means.

Stand with your feet 10 to 15 inches apart and square to the target. The ball should be opposite the toes of your left foot. Remember to flex your knees and balance yourself comfortably, with your weight primarily on your left foot. Place the putter behind the ball and see that the ball is directly below your left eye. You should feel comfortable. Any position that feels unnatural will surely affect your stroke.

Figure 58: *Putting grip (front view).*

Figure 59: *Putting grip (side view).*

Figure 60: *Putting address.*

Now look again at your target and check every part of your setup for proper alignment to the target—target line, putter head, feet, hips, shoulders, hands, and back down to the putter. Now visualize the stroke through the ball. Draw the putter head straight back, allowing it to rise slightly along its natural arc above the green. How far back do you move the blade? Some prefer to maintain a slow controlled rhythm and to stroke the putter head over a greater distance for longer putts, while other golfers prefer to move the putter the same distance each time but strike the ball more firmly to achieve distance. The one that's right is the one that works for you.

Stroke through the ball using the center of the blade and taking great care to keep the putter face square to the target line. While you are doing so, the club, hands, wrists, arms, and shoulders should all move as one pendulumlike unit. Feel that the right hand is controlling the swing while the left is leading the club over the ball. Beginners will find this rigid or pendulum method the easiest way of putting. It has the disadvantage, however, of a limited amount of feel for the putt in the hands. In contrast, many professionals are wrist putters. More seasoned players may like the feel of allowing the wrists to break slightly.

Follow through straight along the target line, allowing the putter to arc upward slightly (see figure 63). As when you drew your club back, your follow-through should continue the pendulumlike motion. Concentrate on the follow-through of your putter head to prevent yourself from looking up too early and spoiling your putt.

Finally, as the ball rolls over the lip, listen to one of the most beautiful sounds in golf: that quiet little cluck the ball makes against the bottom of the cup.

Just as in any other stroke, once you find what works for you, make your preparations into a ritual. Evaluating the green, gripping, aiming, taking your stance and your practice strokes should all be performed in the same way every time. This will help you to putt consistently and therefore successfully.

Figure 61: *Pendulum motion in putting.*

Figure 62: *Contact with the sweet spot of the putter.*

Figure 63: *Absolutely square.*

8. Practice Tips and Exercises

A Few General Tips

Of utmost importance is that you *never* practice while you are playing a game of golf. Don't make modifications to your swing or try new techniques in the midst of a game. What you should be doing during a game is filing away mental notes (or even written ones) about what you might practice next time and, in the meantime, ENJOYING YOURSELF on the course!

For those times when you are *practicing,* this chapter will present some *basic* ideas about golf that have held true over time. These basic principles should be useful throughout your golfing career.

Remember that if you practice anything enough it will become automatic. Don't practice bad habits or they will become automatic. Make sure that you are using correct golfing procedures so that you develop good golfing habits. It is also very important to practice when you are mentally and physically alert. Some freshness is required; by practicing when you are exhausted, you will only end up practicing sloppily. Frequent, short practice sessions will help to improve your golf game more than sporadic, longer ones. In a short session, not only do you remain fresh, but it is easier to set a specific skill-developing goal for that session. An attainable goal provides incentive for the session and offers some sure satisfaction. Even if you don't master a skill in one session, at least you'll progress to the point where you can end on a successful note.

Practicing Exercises

Part of practice should be warming up, just as a little practice and warm-up is not inappropriate before you play. The first thing you should do is warm up and stretch your back and shoulder muscles, maybe by holding two or three clubs and gently swinging them. Or you can hold or lock a club behind your back with your elbows and twist. Then, take up your stance and shift your weight from foot to foot just as you would during the backswing, swing, and follow-through, rotating your hips naturally. Then, using an imaginary golf ball and clubs, extend your arms out from your sides and twist your trunk so you can point at the ball alternately with your extended right and left hands.

Figure 64: *Always loosen up before playing a round.*

Figure 65: *There are many ways to stretch.*

Figure 66: *Visualize a perfect swing.*

While at the practice range, check your aim by aligning a club alongside the ball parallel to your imagined target line. Take your stance and check it by setting a second club down on the ground so that the shaft touches the tips of both shoes. The two clubs should be parallel. Next, address the ball, see that the blade of the club is at right angles to the two shafts on the ground. Now pick up the clubs and start hitting a few balls with your pitching wedge, not hard, just to get everything working together. Work your way down through the set, not going for distance, just warming up; start off with the more forgiving clubs and finish with the more exacting long irons and woods.

After you've hit a few balls with each club, work your way back up the set, using a full swing and simulating the order of clubs you might use in a game.

Figure 67: *He's working to "groove" his swing.*

Remember, even on the practice range, always aim for a target. It's a great opportunity to become familiar with your own capabilities, both the likelihood that you will hit the ball accurately and the sort of distance *you* can expect out of a given club.

Then head on over to the putting green near the first tee, toss a few balls in the bunker and pitch them onto the green. Chip a few more on from the rough, then see if you can't manage to two-putt them all, concentrating on distance on your first putts. If you're having trouble keeping your putter face square to the target line, set your balls 18 inches from the hole and one at a time address the balls, resting your putter up against them. Now, using your putting stroke without backswing, push the balls into the cup, following through straight across the hole. Soon you'll be draining your putts with ease.

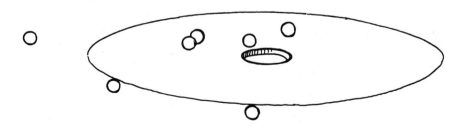

Figure 68: *Two-putt practice.*

9. Diagnostics

A good swing develops over time with many correct, repetitive swings of the club. Essential to a good, sound swing is a correct setup before the club has even moved an inch.

Alignment

The best order of preparation is to aim your club, then set your grip, and then step into your stance. This makes sense if you consider that the clubhead is easy to move and your stance takes a good deal more effort to adjust. If you set your stance first, a hook or slice will probably be the result. Train yourself to align the clubhead first and then take your grip and stance.

Ball Position

Even if your feet are aligned properly, if the ball is out of position in relation to your feet the club will not swing straight through the ball along the target line. If the ball is too far forward, it will cramp the backswing and very little distance will come from that swing. If the ball is too far back, the swing itself will be cramped and will angle from "in to out," sending the ball careening off to the right. (For the proper way to position the ball, see page 17.)

Grip

Grip problems generally take four forms: left hand under the handle, left hand over the handle, right hand under the handle, right hand over the handle, or a combination of these. They are illustrated in figures 69 through 72.

Left hand under: If the left hand is positioned too far under the club, the back of the hand will be facing the body, not the target. During the swing the left hand will turn to the correct position, forcing the clubface to open to the right. The result will be a slice.

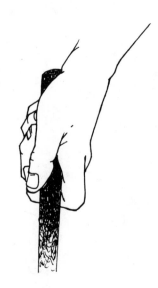

Figure 69: *A weak left-hand grip.*

Left hand over: The same natural return to the correct position will happen when the back of the left hand is facing away from the body. During the swing it will close the clubface to the left, and the ball will hook off into the trees or the left side of the fairway.

Figure 70: *A strong left-hand grip.*

Right hand over: If the right hand is positioned too far on top of the handle, it, too, will rotate during the swing to its correct position. This will open the clubface and result in a slice into the water hazard off to the right.

Figure 71: *A weak right-hand grip.*

Right hand under: If the right hand is positioned too far under the handle, palm facing outward, as it gravitates to the correct position during the swing, it will turn the clubface inward, creating another hook shot.

(For a description of the correct grip, see pages 12–14.)

Figure 72: *An improper "beginner's grip."*

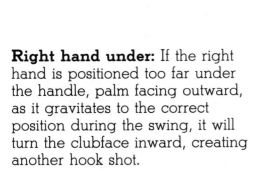

Alignment

If, in taking your position, you don't manage to align the toes of your shoes with the target line, but instead line up "open," with your left shoulder and foot back from the line, then a ball hit squarely to your feet will travel to the left of target (line A in figure 73). If, while swinging from this position, you manage to square the clubface with the target line, the ball will slice to the right (line B in figure 73, and also figure 74).

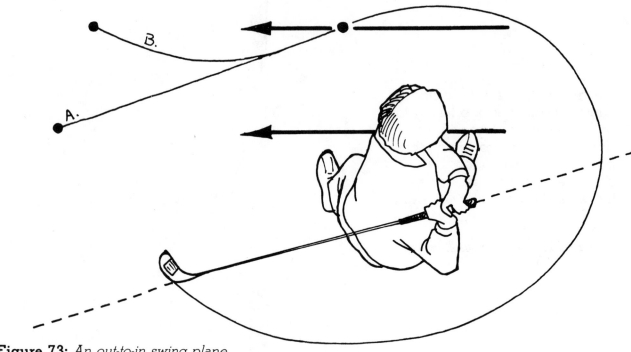

Figure 73: *An out-to-in swing plane.*

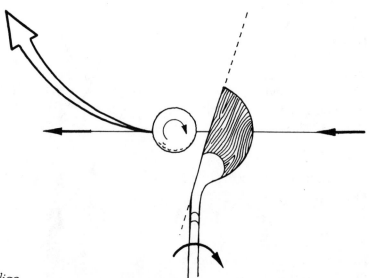

Figure 74: *Mechanics of the slice.*

If, on the other hand, your stance is closed, and you are actually facing slightly away from the target, the ball will obviously travel to the right of your target if you swing square to your feet (line A in figure 75). If the clubhead is closed, so that it lines up with the pin, you'll hook the ball left (line B in figure 75, and figure 76).

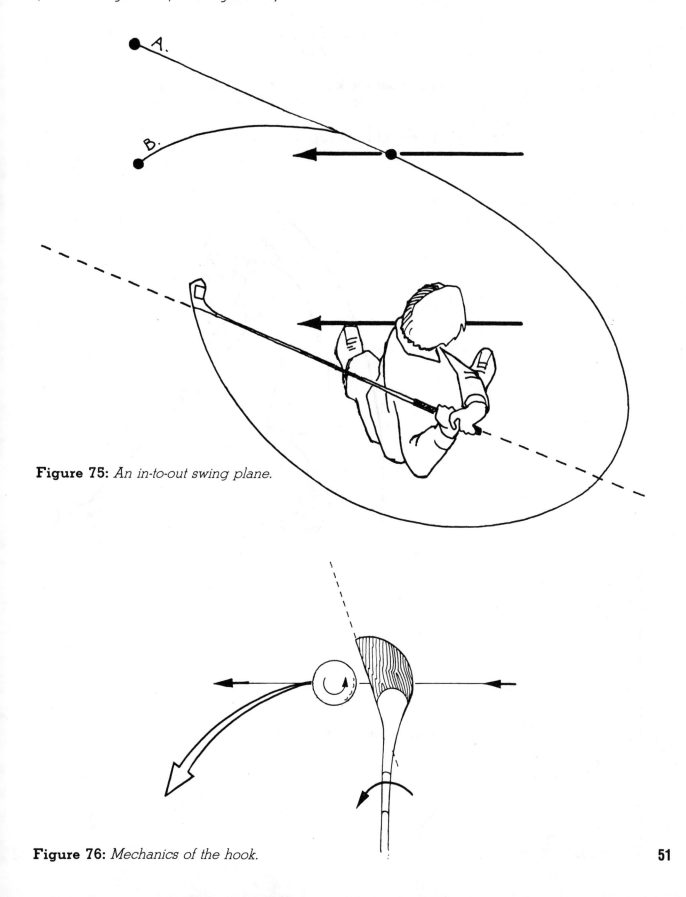

Figure 75: *An in-to-out swing plane.*

Figure 76: *Mechanics of the hook.*

Posture

If you find yourself hunching over and reaching for the ball with your club while your legs strain to maintain your balance, you are positioned too far away from the ball. In this position, your head will inevitably move during the swing. If you do hit the ball, you will hit it weakly because your legs (whose large muscles help power your shots) will be busy keeping you from falling forward.

Setting up too close to the ball so your back is ramrod straight, with your weight on your heels, will make it very difficult to hit the ball at all, since your swing plane is so upright.

Even if you set up correctly, other problems can develop as the swing progresses.

Figure 77: *The ball is too far away, so the posture is too hunched over.*

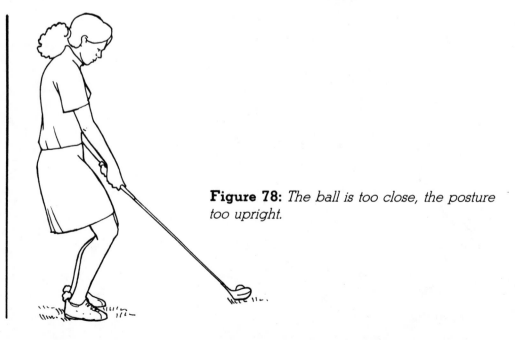

Figure 78: *The ball is too close, the posture too upright.*

Swaying occurs when a golfer moves his upper body laterally during the backswing. You can spot swaying by being aware of the focus of your left eye on the ball during the backswing. Coordinating the shoulder, arm, and wrist movements of the backswing will help you avoid swaying.

Figure 79: *Sway. Notice the shift of the head away from above the ball.*

Sometimes, your arms and club seem to get ahead of the rest of your body, leaving your legs and hips behind so they cannot contribute any of their power to the swing. Sometimes the swing is all arms and no hip turn at all. To remedy this, as you complete your backswing, replant your left heel, which should have risen slightly on the backswing; think of this as the trigger for both your downswing and your weight shift from right (rear) to left. The same emphasis on footwork will help the golfer who tends to put weight on the right (rear) leg during the follow-through. Placing the weight on the insides of the feet and slightly widening the stance may help, too.

Although many professional golfers have altered their swing planes in one way or another, it is important that golfers match the angle of their swing planes to their physiques. A shorter golfer will have a flatter swing plane and a taller golfer, a more upright one. A swing plane that is too flat for your height will tend to push the ball into that bunker on the right of the fairway; a too-upright swing plane will cause a slice with the longer shafted clubs and a hook with the shorter ones.

Figure 80: *Arms getting ahead of hip turn.*

Figure 81: *Lack of hip turn.*

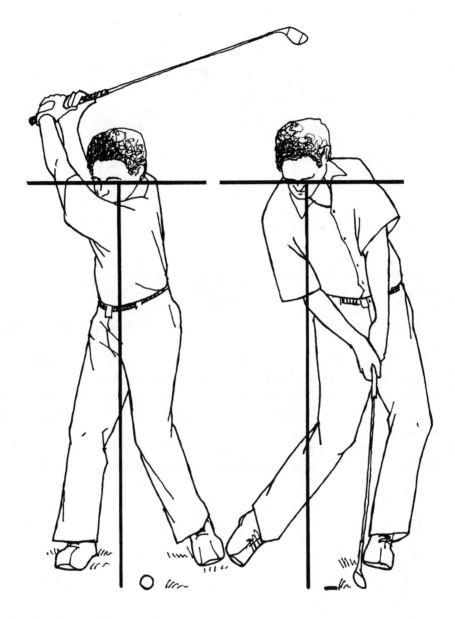

Figure 82: *Keeping the head down and steady.*

It's true that PGA players watch the ball during their follow-through. They rotate their heads at the neck and *turn,* not lift, their heads. Not primarily to watch the ball, rather it is a natural part of their swinging motion and makes room for a full follow-through. Non-professional players, on the other hand, can hardly help but jerk (not rotate) their heads up, usually before they've even hit the ball. If a golfer jerks his or her head up, up go the shoulders, too, and along with the shoulders comes the clubhead. It hits the top half of the ball, which then rolls along the ground. So here's some old-fashioned, common sense advice: concentrate on the ball, keep your head down, and look at the spot the ball left even after you're sure the ball is away.

10. Rules and Etiquette

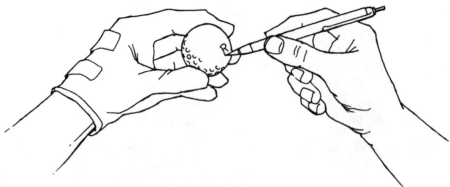

Figure 83: *Mark your ball to avoid confusion.*

All golfers understand the one basic concept behind the rules of golf: play it as it lays. That idea and common sense seem like enough rule knowledge for most players. In general, it is enough. This chapter, however, will provide you with a few additional basic guidelines which will help you play within the rules.

First, before teeing off, be sure you can identify your ball. This will be helpful if two balls land near each other or if your ball gets lost.

Let the golfer with the lowest handicap go first on the first hole—this is not a rule, but a courtesy. On all following holes the low scorer from the previous hole goes first.

After everyone has taken a tee shot, who goes first on the second shot? The person farthest from the hole. That helps your group keep together as

Figure 84: *Stroke and distance; in this case, "three from the tee."*

you move from ball to ball through the fairway. But what if your tee shot dropped into the middle of the lake? Your fellow golfer may tell you to "take a mulligan," which means you should take a second tee shot and not count the first one. It's totally illegal, since you are not allowed to take practice shots, but offering a mulligan is a nice thing to do in a social game of golf.

Legally you would take what is commonly called "stroke and distance." This is applied frequently when your ball goes out of bounds, is lost, or gets stuck in a tree. For stroke and distance you add a penalty stroke to your score and go back to the spot where you originally played, and play a new ball. So, counting your first tee shot, your penalty stroke, and your second tee shot, your score now totals three.

Say your next shot (you'll go next since you are farthest from the pin) ends up in the deep rough. Remember, you've got to play the course as you find it. This rule applies most strongly to hazards, such as cattails on the edge of a pond, or to sand traps. In these hazards you are not ever allowed to touch the club to the ground or "ground" the club until you actually hit the ball.

So your next shot hooks wickedly back over the fairway and continues on out of bounds. Just like water hazards, out-of-bounds areas are usually marked by stakes. At this point, it's stroke-and-distance time again, so you go back to the rough where you shot the ball. (By the way, you're allowed to stand out of bounds to hit a ball that's in bounds.) You can't tee up or place

Figure 85: *An illegal improvement of the lie.*

Figure 86: *This sort of practice swing is not allowed.*

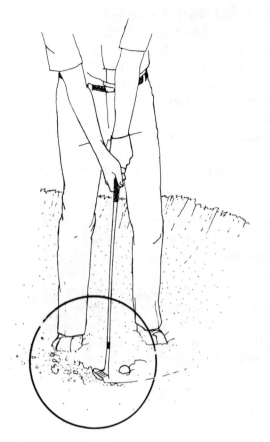

Figure 87: *Never ground your club in a hazard.*

Figure 89: *Proper form for dropping the ball.*

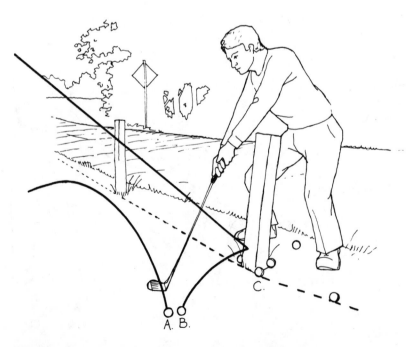

Figure 88: *Balls A and B and C may be played; all others are out of bounds.*

the ball, but must "drop" it. Stand and hold the ball at shoulder height and drop it; you may face in any direction you like. The ball may not, however, touch you or your clothing before or after it hits the ground. If it does, it must be redropped, but there's no penalty for that. Make sure it doesn't roll more than two club lengths away or you'll have to do it again. If your dropped ball goes into a hazard (or out of the one you are in), onto a green, out of bounds, back where it was or more than two club lengths from where it was, or nearer to the hole than it was, then you must redrop it, without penalty. If it rolls too far again, place it as near the original location as you can. After this moderately disastrous start, you'd like to get to the green as quickly as possible, but we need to cover a few more points first.

During the course of a round you may remove "loose impediments" that interfere with play—typically something like a pinecone.

You can play a second, "provisional" ball if you suspect yours may be lost. When you reach the spot where it entered the jungle, take five minutes to look for your original ball. If you find it, you can play it without penalty. If you can't find the ball, you can continue with the provisional, adding three strokes to your total. This is another way of playing stroke and distance, but saving yourself a two-way, 200-yard march to play it.

You can declare any ball unplayable and take a one-stroke penalty. You then have three options: drop the ball up to two club lengths away from the unplayable lie, but no nearer to the pin; drop the ball on a line that runs straight back from the pin through the unplayable lie; or drop the ball back at the spot from which you played it. Choose whichever option seems to give you the greatest advantage and be careful how you drop the ball. If it rolls into another unplayable lie, that's your tough luck.

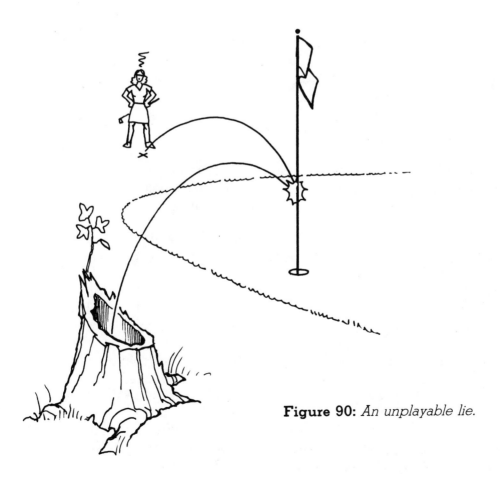

Figure 90: *An unplayable lie.*

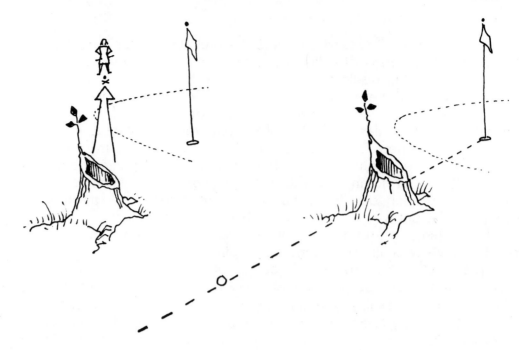

Figure 91: *The golfer's three options in an unplayable lie.*

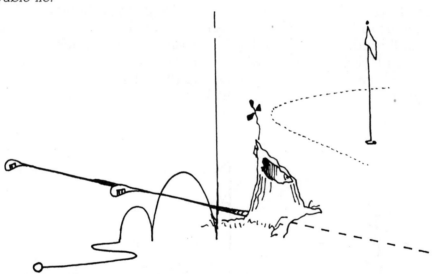

You may move an obstruction such as a dead branch on the ground (as long as it isn't in a hazard), or if you can't move the obstruction (for example, a parked tractor), then you can drop without penalty two club lengths away from the obstruction.

You may also drop without penalty for relief from a puddle that was not intended as a hazard or drop from "ground under repair" at the nearest spot that provides relief.

Remember the tractor? Well, the grounds keeper just drove it over your ball. You can place the ball as near as possible to the original spot. The tractor, or even another player who accidentally kicks your ball, is known as an "outside agent"; you play without penalty.

Don't worry if an alligator chews your ball—any damaged ball may be replaced. On the other hand, don't hope for a miracle fifty-miles-per-hour gust of wind to blow your 37-foot putt into the cup before you even touch it. You can only wait a few seconds for a ball on the lip of the cup to topple in.

The rules for the putting green differ in many respects from the fairway rules. This is because the putting game stresses rolling the ball and because of the delicate nature of the green itself.

You may remove loose impediments such as grass clippings or dead leaves anywhere along the line of your putt. Don't test the grass while doing so, however; that's illegal. Also, if your ball, your ball's path, or your stance are affected by "casual water" you may move the ball and place it at the *nearest* point which will give you relief, as long as it's not nearer the hole.

You may also lift the ball from the green to clean it or to remove it at your partner's request when it is obstructing his or her path to the cup. Place a marker first. Use something like a coin for the marker; place it on the spot, or if necessary, two putter-head lengths away. A marker helps you replace the ball accurately.

Figure 92: *Illegal testing of the green.*

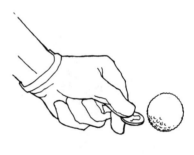

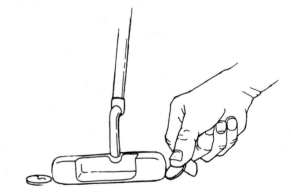

Figure 94: *Two methods of marking the ball.*

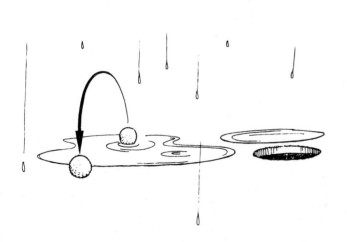

Figure 93: *Relief from casual water on the green.*

A couple of points to remember: if you land on the wrong green you should not pitch from there and put a gash the size of a second hole in the green. Instead, drop your ball off the green with no penalty.

Always attend to the flag when your friends are putting. Although you are allowed to hit the flag when you play from the fairway, if you hit it while putting there's a stiff two-stroke or loss-of-hole penalty.

This is by no means a complete list of the rules of golf. Hundreds of points are covered in the official rules. This will, I hope, be enough to impart a basic feel for the spirit of the rules and give you the confidence to handle situations as they arise.

Most golfing courtesy is just plain old-fashioned good manners. Not all golfing etiquette is entirely self-explanatory; therefore a few points need to be raised.

With the exception of some galleries at major golfing events, just about everyone is aware that talking while a player is making a stroke is bad manners. So is moving around or standing in a player's line of vision.

It's expected that you wait to play your ball until the group ahead of you is well out of range.

Figure 95: *A one-in-a-thousand hook shot.*

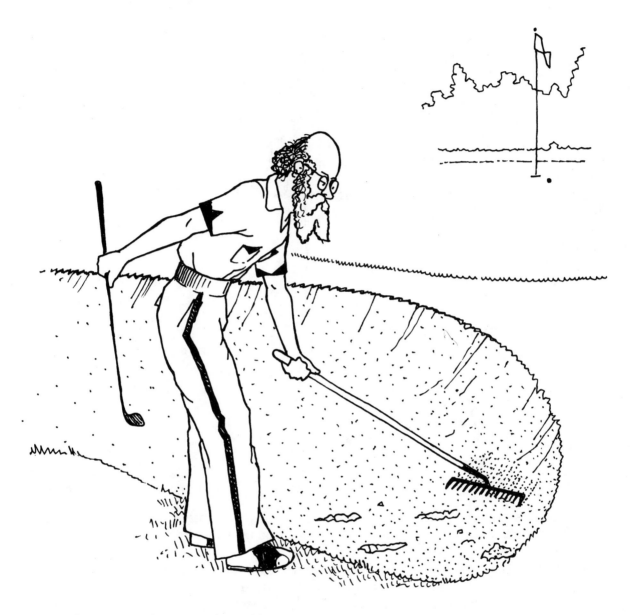

Figure 96: *Smooth the footprints from the bunker.*

You should leave the course as you found it. If possible, replace any divots that you take and rake your footprints out of the sand traps. There may be a rake nearby; if not, smooth out the sand with your club. After all, how would *you* like to peer over the edge to find that not only have you landed in a bunker, but in a minibunker within a bunker that was made by some elephantine golfer?

Figure 97: *Avoid slow play by being ready for your turn.*

   Slow play is one of the principal complaints that golfers have about each other. To help avoid this, take your practice swings in a way that won't hold up or distract the other members of your party. After your shot, make a note of where your ball has settled, using a landmark such as a tree, then walk briskly toward it. Although it's not thoughtful to play as if you were uninterested in your friends' shots, you should be ready to hit when it's your turn. Even if you need to stand slightly ahead of them on the fairway, it's all right as long as you are not in the line of fire or distracting them.
   Follow the proper order of hitting on the tee: the low scorer from the previous hole goes first. During play, the person farthest from the flag goes first.
   If you are having a hard time keeping station with the golfers ahead of you, and you are holding up golfers behind you, wave through the players behind you so they won't have to wait for you. When at the green, place your clubs off the green so after you finish you can leave at once. Wait until you've left to start marking your scorecard.
   If you are having trouble reading the green (which you should begin doing long before you reach it), then by all means pace, squat, use the plumb-bob method (as described on pages 40–41), or anything else. But please, do this as quickly and efficiently as possible. Keep in mind that many golfers firmly believe that a brisk pace improves their game.

It's thoughtless to damage the green with your equipment. Don't set your bag on the green or pull your cart across it. Never drive across the green. If you are wearing spikes, pick your feet up, don't shuffle, and repair any pitch marks you make.

Remember, the most delicate part of the green is the hole. Don't step on or near its edges or it will develop a maddening moat around it. Also be careful with the edges of the hole as you take up and replace the flag.

Distracting a playing partner by walking across the line of his putt is another example of bad golfing manners. It's even considered bad form to cast a shadow across the line of the putt.

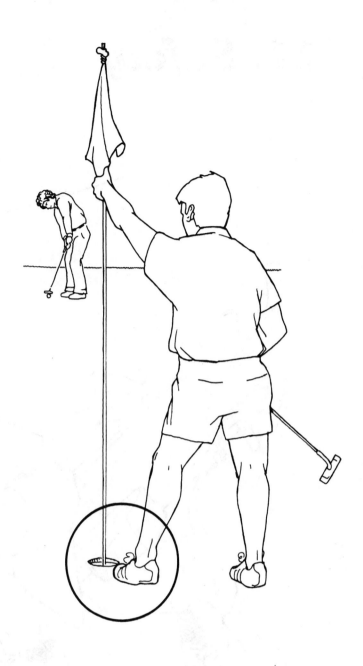

Figure 98: *Repetitive stepping near the hole damages the green, and distracts the golfer who is putting.*

Always mark and remove your ball when there's a chance it might interfere with another player's putt. A partner can insist you lift and mark it, but he shouldn't have to ask. Remove your ball from the cup immediately after holing out.

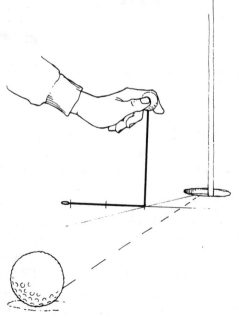

Figure 99: *Lifting the ball to give a partner room to putt.*

11. Safety

Figure 100: *When you hear "fore!"—believe it.*

The cardinal rule of safety is: do not take a shot if there is *any chance* you might hit someone with it. If, however, it looks like your ball might hit someone after you have swung, you should shout, "Fore!" Do it *loudly* and do it *immediately.*

If you hear the cry of "fore!" you have two choices: you can turn around to gape at whoever shouted and risk getting your teeth knocked out by a golf ball, or you can duck and cover. I recommend the latter.

Never approach a golfer from the rear when he is addressing the ball or taking practice swings, unless, of course, you enjoy that kicked-by-a-mule sensation. By the same token, don't swing a club when anyone is standing nearby—sweaty hands have been known to slip.

Figure 101: *Walking behind a golfer when he is addressing the ball is both impolite and unwise.*

Don't take chances in extreme weather. Next time you're playing Augusta National, remember it gets hot down south, so be sure to drink plenty . . . of *water.*

A word to the wise: lightning doesn't shout "fore!" In the United States alone, thousands of people are killed by lightning every year, and some of them are always golfers. When the weather looks dicey, ditch the expensive set of clubs and the umbrella (both natural lightning rods) and take shelter in dense woods, a depression, or by lying flat on the ground. Some survivors of lightning-strikes had some warning, others never saw it coming.

Golf carts: walk. Stay out of them if you possibly can. If you can't give them up, stay all the way in them; crushed ankles are the most common golf-cart injury.

Figure 102: *Some people need golf carts. But walking generally improves the rhythm of a golfer's overall game and stroke.*

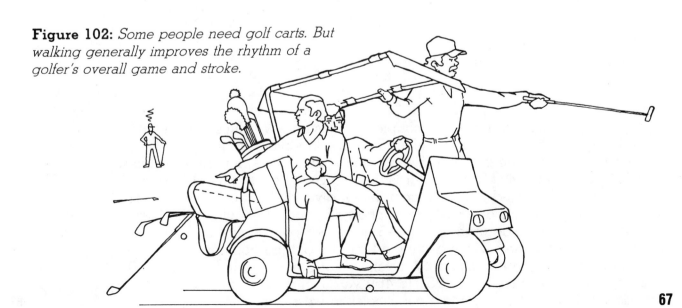

12. Forms of Play

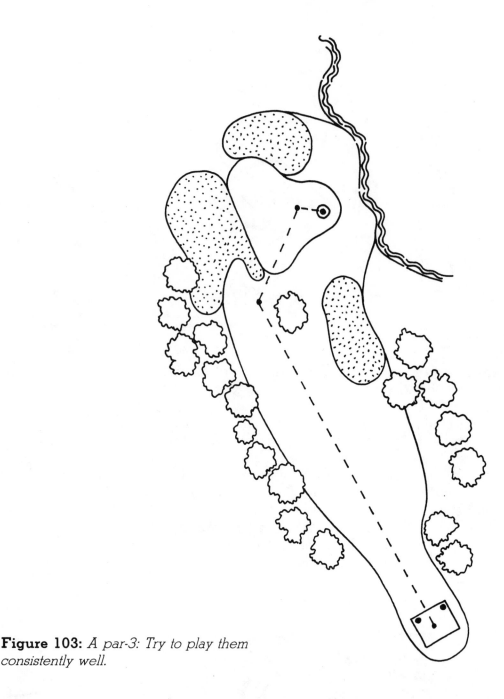

Figure 103: *A par-3: Try to play them consistently well.*

Although you and I might play a couple of holes on a Wednesday evening, golf is by definition an eighteen-hole game divided into a front nine holes and a back nine. Each of the eighteen holes is assigned a number of strokes according to its length. This number is the number of strokes a very good golfer can be expected to take to complete a given hole. It is known as par. Although layout varies drastically from one golf course to another, the best courses are often made up of four par-3 holes, ten par-4 holes, and four par-5 holes, which are evenly distributed throughout the golf course. Par on each of the holes is determined by distance. Par-3 holes are as long as 250 yards, par-4 holes range from 251 to 469 yards, and par-5 holes are 469 yards and longer. There are few par-6 holes in existence.

The green on a par-3 hole should be reached by a really good golfer in one stroke. Then normally the golfer would two-putt, making a total of three strokes. The much longer par-5 would require three strokes to reach the green, and again the two putts make a total of five strokes.

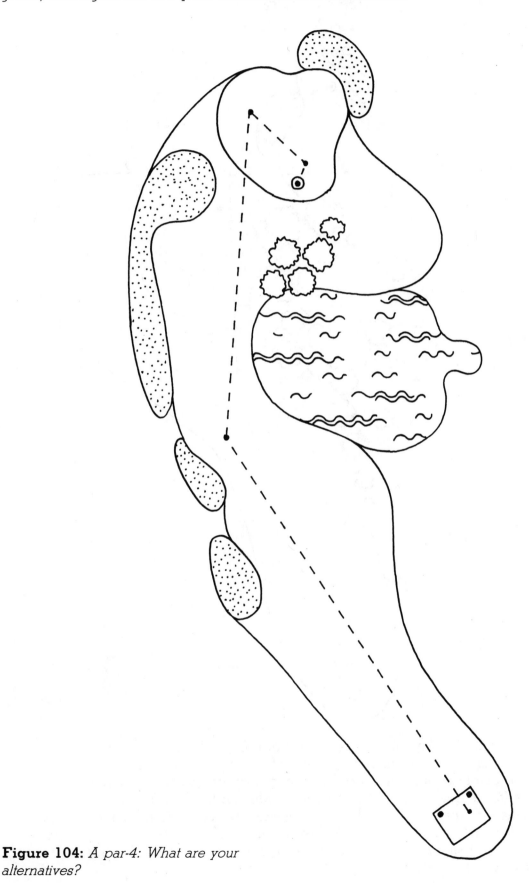

Figure 104: *A par-4: What are your alternatives?*

Figure 105: *A par-5: Your chance for an eagle.*

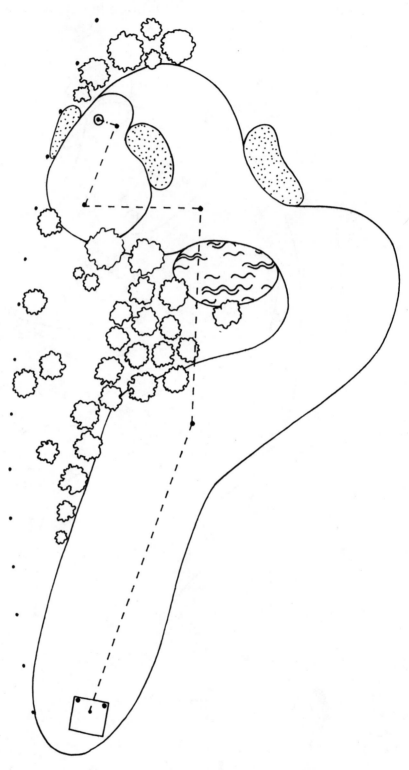

A golfer who is able to play all eighteen holes at par would have played a "scratch" round, and could rightfully call himself or herself a scratch golfer. There are plenty of times a good golfer might go one stroke over par on the first hole (for a "bogey"), and one stroke under on the next hole (a "birdie"), and then on the third hole the golfer makes two strokes under for an "eagle," and on the fourth, two strokes over for a "double-bogey." Therefore, this golfer has a scratch score for the overall game without having shot par on any hole.

Most golfers, however, never consistently achieve this level of play and are given a rating known as a handicap. The handicapping system is one of the reasons golf has had such great success. It enables relative novices to play with the most accomplished golfers, and do so with a near even chance of victory. Basically, a handicap is obtained by submitting three official scorecards for rounds played over approved courses to the club's handicapping committee. The three total scores are averaged and par for the course (72) is subtracted from it. The resulting number is that golfer's handicap. The maximum handicap for men is 28 and for women 36. Handicaps are used in different ways to put everyone on an equal competitive footing, depending on the type of match being played.

YDS	434	365	265	213	418	301	50	166	428	3101	YDS	527	292	471	143	203	396	321	427	387	3180	6281	
PAR	5	4	4	3	4	4	5	3	4	36	PAR	5	4	5	3	3	4	4	4	4	36	72	
HOLE	1	2	3	4	5	6	7	8	9	OUT	HOLE	10	11	12	13	14	15	16	17	18	IN		
HDCP	11	5	13	9	1	15	7	17	3		HDCP	8	16	6	18	10	2	14	4	12			
P.B.	7	6	4	7	8	3	8	5	7	55		8	6	7	5	6	7	5	7	6	57	112	
ANNE	7	4	5	4	7	4	6	4	8	49		8	5	6	4	5	6	6	7	5	52	101	

Figure 106: *A typical scorecard.*

There are two basic forms of play: stroke play, which has become the most common and popular, and match play, which is the older form.

In stroke play the golfer is playing more against the course or against par than he is against an opponent. All the holes must be completed and then the total number of strokes are added up. The golfer's assigned handicap is then deducted and that number is his or her final score.

This type of match, which a golfer can play alone or against a large field of other golfers, can be modified into a foursome. Two partners compete against two other golfers, the partners taking alternate strokes on their one ball and teeing off at alternate holes. After their round they subtract one-half their combined handicaps.

The *Scotch foursome* is played when both partners tee off, pick the best ball, and play it alternately. It's played against another pair of golfers and at the end of the round, three-eighths of the sum of the team's handicaps is subtracted from the score.

In *Stableford golf,* par is used as a basis for awarding points. On a given hole, one point is awarded for one over par, two points for a score of one under par, and three for an eagle. Handicaps are deducted hole by hole, as listed on the scorecard. The advantage for the novice with more than one over par on a given hole is to be able to simply pick up the ball, take zero points and move on to the next hole, even if he or she shot three balls into the lake.

The other basic form of play is match play. This is golf played against an opponent on a hole-by-hole basis. It continues until one player is up by more holes than there are left to play. Handicap allowances are printed on a hole-by-hole basis on the scorecard.

Match play can also be played in the form of fourball, where each golfer plays his or her own ball and the two teammates take the score of their best ball. The result is decided by whichever team wins the most holes. The three highest handicaps are each calculated at three-quarters the difference between their official handicap and the lowest handicapper in the group. As always, hole-by-hole allowances are listed on the scorecard.

13. Strategy and Tactics

Once you develop a stroke you can depend on, and so have some degree of control over the ball, you can begin to think about strategy and tactics. The two basic competitive structures in golf, stroke play and match play, have corresponding strategic mind-sets. Stroke play is cumulative. It is all about consistency over eighteen holes and biding your time until an opportunity presents itself. It's about playing against the course and against yourself.

Match play, on the other hand, is about having the nerve and common sense to take appropriate risks and advantage of your opponent to win holes. In match play, if you take a risk and it doesn't work out, it may cost you the hole. But you've still got seventeen more to go. In stroke play if you take a risk and go four over on the first hole, those four strokes will haunt you for the rest of the afternoon. That's why in stroke play it is important to examine the course and develop a game plan ahead of time, and then stick with the game plan. Remember that a round was never lost by one particular stroke, nor was it won by one, so if you make a mistake, don't give up, but don't take undue risks. Chances to one-putt will come to those who wait for them.

In match play you can just about forget about par. Tailor your game toward winning the hole. If your opponent has to take stroke and distance on his tee shot, don't do him or her the favor of doing the same. A nice conservative, controlled shot to the middle of the fairway will do the trick—who cares if you win the hole at one over par. You won it, didn't you? Conversely, if your opponent is on the green in two on a par-4 and looks like he or she is going to hole out with the next stroke, it doesn't make sense to play a nice cautious approach shot you know you can make, then chip and run, and one-putt since you've already lost the hole. You've got to go for the flag right away, even if it means out of the rough, under a branch, and over a sand trap.

Tactics

A little common sense and intelligence will go a long way toward cutting strokes off your game. Golf course architects get paid a lot of money. And what the great ones get paid for is not so much building golf courses as it is *challenging* golfers. So, the first thing to do before teeing off is to survey the hole and try to figure out how the designer is trying to challenge you. What choices are being offered?

Before just bashing your tee shot, anticipate. Know the location of the pin and the hazards that surround it. Aim your drive and it may make your approach shot a lot easier. Then, calculate the benefits of any reasonable risk. For example, if you've got a dogleg hole and you're considering cutting the corner over the trees, will you really benefit if your approach is then blocked by a near-side bunker?

What if you play it conservatively, only to discover your second shot must now wing over Lake Wallapatuka? Take the time to figure out what kind of a gambit you are being offered. And in match play, consider your handicap

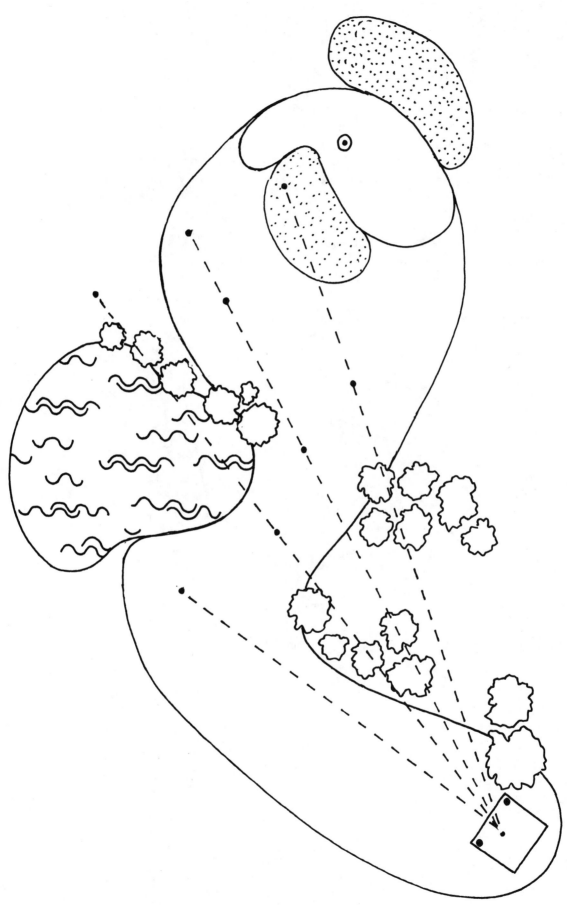

Figure 107: *Consider your second shot before teeing off.*

for the given hole. If this is the kind of tough hole that will give you a stroke, then what can you do with it?

After considering your options, tee up. If a hole has a danger, say a river running along the left side, you may be tempted to tee up as far away from it as possible. (You should also be aware that the teeing ground may have more than one set of markers designating the line behind which players must tee up the ball. Red markers closer to the green are for ladies; white ones farthest from the hole are for championship use only; the yellow ones are for everyone else.) Unfortunately, teeing up away from the danger virtually assures hitting toward the danger. You should line up your tee shot on the near side and then you'll be guaranteed to hit away from the fish.

Figure 108: *"A" seems to be away from danger, but is a poor choice; "B" seems nearer to danger, but is the better choice.*

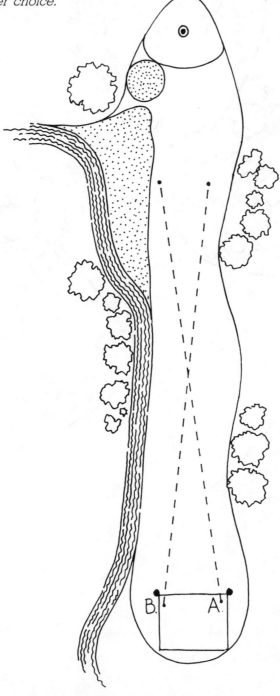

If you haven't conquered your slice yet on the practice range, then don't fight it during the match. Expect it, use it! Then go to work on it next week *on the practice range.*

Remember, on wet days you don't have distance, so get the ball well up in the air and strive for accuracy. The last thing you want to do is end up in the rough in wet weather.

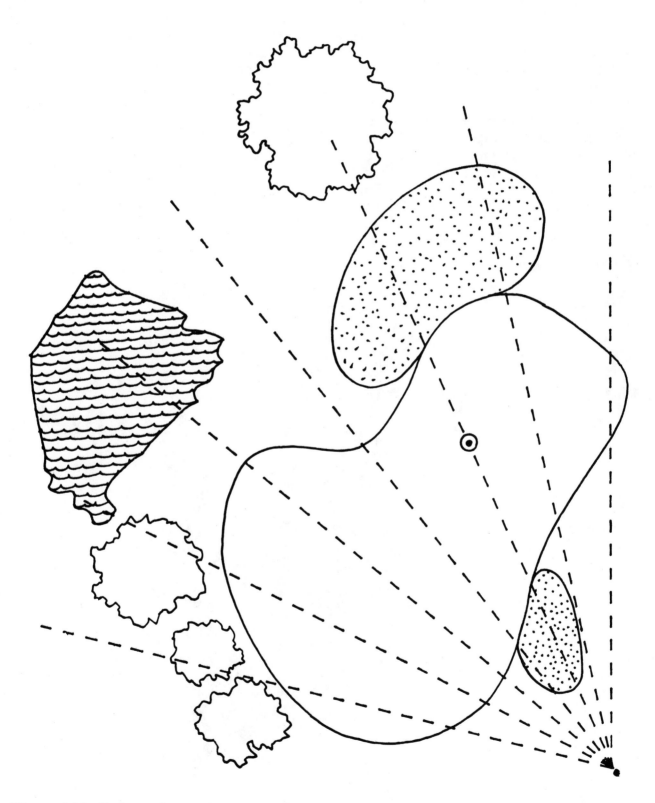

Figure 109: *Evaluate the consequences of error, but visualize success during the stroke.*

Stay away from water. If you land in a sand trap in back of the green, you've got a challenge. If you land in the water in front of it, you've got a one-stroke penalty and a drop that could leave you with a pretty tough challenge anyway.

But don't let water you must cross rattle you. You've developed a consistent stroke, remember? Just choose your target intelligently, focus on it mentally, tune out the water entirely, and swing confidently.

After you have developed a consistent stroke, you are more likely to slice or hook into trouble than top the ball into it. So don't skirt a problem when you can go right over it.

When taking a shot consider the consequences of a poor stroke. If the outcome looks bleak, alter your target to avoid it and you'll swing with confidence.

In conclusion, let me leave you with this: heather. Heather is that nasty Scottish vegetation, a plant that eats golf balls and snares golf clubs that try to swing through it, much like a spider snares flies. Ironically, or maybe it shows the special mental attitude of the committed golfer, this stuff is considered good luck in sprig form, when attached to the golf bag. Find some. Pin a piece to your bag. Good luck!

Figure 110:

Glossary

Ace A hole in one.

Address Positioning of oneself and the club in preparation for the swing.

Apron The grass that borders the green, usually mowed shorter than the fairway, but not as short as the green.

Arc The semicircular swing path of the clubhead.

Attending the flag Taking up and holding the flag for your fellow players as they try to hole out.

Back marker The player in a round with the lowest handicap, i.e., the best player.

Backspin The spin of the ball in the opposite direction from the one it is traveling. The amount of spin, fast or slow, is determined by the loft of the club.

Backswing The movement of the club up and behind the body prior to the swing.

Baffy An old-fashioned wooden club most similar to today's 4-wood.

Best ball A type of game where the lowest score of two partners is the one that is counted.

Birdie One stroke below par.

Bisque An extra handicap stroke, which may be taken at any time during play.

Blade The face of an iron clubhead.

Blaster A wedge with a broad sole.

Block Failing to clear the hips during the swing. The result is that the club strikes the ball in an open position and the ball veers to the right.

Bogey One stroke more than par; double-bogey is two more, triple-bogey, three.

Brassie What is now called a 2-wood.

Bulger A convex-faced driver.

Bunker A hazard, specifically a depression filled with sand.

Caddie The person who carries the golfer's bag, and may also give advice.

Carry The length of a ball's passage through the air before it strikes ground.

Casual water A temporary accumulation of water, which includes snow, ice, or a puddle.

Chip/Chip-and-run A shot intended to send the ball in the air a short distance, after which it lands and rolls. Usually played close to the green.

Closed stance The right foot and right side of the body are drawn back from being parallel to the target line.

Cock The preparatory flex of the left wrist/hinge of the right wrist in the backswing.

Cut Any shot, fade or slice, that moves the ball from left to right through the air.

Divot A hunk of sod taken from the ground by a player's club.

Double-eagle Three strokes below par.

Dub A poor golfer or a bad shot.

Duffer A poor golfer.

Eagle Two strokes below par.

Explosion A shot taken in the sand where the club makes impact with the sand behind the ball.

Extension The stretch of the arms during the follow-through.

Fade A gentle slice spin intended to make the ball stop where it lands.

Fairway The mown length of grass between tee and green.

Flag The movable pole and flag that rests in the hole to mark it.

Flange The extension on the sole of iron clubs.

Fluffing The club making contact with the ground before the ball.

Follow-through The finish of the swing after the ball is struck.

Fourball A match of four players where one team's best ball is played against the other team's.

Foursome A match of four players where teammates take alternate shots at one ball and tee off at alternate holes.

Gimmee A ball that has gotten so close to the hole that the last stroke is a formality.

Grain The direction the grass grows on the putting green.

Green The putting surface.

Ground under repair Any material that is to be removed from the course; this should be marked.

Handicap A number of strokes, based on a player's ability, subtracted from his or her score; the result should be par.

Hanging lie The ball is on sufficiently sloping ground that the player must take an uneven stance.

Hazards Any "natural" obstacles, such as ditches, bunkers, ponds, trees, and bushes; the rules state specifically that hazards include bunkers and water hazards.

Heel The innermost part of the club sole; a shot struck by this area of a wooden club.

Hole The sunken cup on the green that must be reached for completion of that hole.

Hole in one A tee shot that makes the hole.

Honor The right to take the first tee shot on a given hole.

Hook A stroke that inadvertently causes the ball to veer left.

Hosel The place on iron clubs where shaft ends and blade begins.

Interlock A grip where the lower hand locks with the forefinger of the upper hand.

Lie Where the ball comes to rest during play. Also refers to the angle of the clubhead in relation to the shaft.

Line of play/The line The route of a hole that most players use.

Links A golf course, originally used just to describe seaside courses.

Lob A high shot with a lofted club; optimally this shot has little backspin and lands gently.

Local rules Rules at a particular golf course that cover peculiarities of that course.

Loft The angle of a clubface; also, the height of a ball's flight.

Loose impediments Pinecones, twigs, rocks, etc., that are not fixed.

Majors Four championships: The Masters; The U.S. Open; The British Open; and The PGA Championship.

Marker The person who keeps score; also, the coin, etc., put down to mark the position of a ball moved temporarily out of another player's way.

Match play A competition where each hole is a separate contest; the player who wins the most holes wins the match.

Mixed foursome Two men and two women.

Mulligan A free second drive when the first one is bad. Offering a mulligan is an unofficial practice among friendly players.

Nap The grain of the grass on the green.

Nassau A three-part wager, on the front nine, back nine, and overall match.

Obstruction Any artificial object erected, placed, or abandoned on the course. Fences, roads, tractors, utility boxes all qualify.

Open stance The left foot and left side of the body are drawn back from being parallel to the target line.

Out of bounds Any area outside the designated markers.

Outside agent Any nonplayer at a match, including refs, markers, observers, or competitors not involved in the actual game. Also includes alligators, deer, cows, etc.

Overlap The earliest form of the Vardon grip.

Par The normal score of very good players, usually set according to the length of the hole.

Penalty A stroke added for breaking a rule.

Pitch A shot that floats high, often to a green.

Pivot The turn of the body in the backswing.

Press To double an existing bet in the midst of play.

Rough Deep grass and other vegetation on the borders of the fairway.

Scotch foursome A kind of hybrid of fourball and foursome, in which the players on a team both drive, and then take alternate shots at the best ball.

Scratch player A zero-handicap player who generally hits par.

Setup The aiming and body positioning preparatory to taking the swing.

Singles Two golfers playing together.

Skull A glancing blow to the ball.

Slice A shot that veers to the right.

Smother The club hits the ball, but with too little loft to lift it.

Sole The bottom of the club; also, to rest the sole on the ground at address.

Square stance The body is parallel to the ball–target line.

Stableford Type of golf where a score of par earns one point; one stroke under par earns two points; two under, three points; and so on. High score wins.

Stance The position of the player in relation to

the ball immediately prior to the swing.

Stroke Forward movement of the club with the intention of striking the ball.

Stroke play A type of play where the total strokes for a round are counted.

Swing plane The path of the club around the player during the swing.

Takeaway The beginning of the backswing.

Target line The straight line running through ball and target.

Tee The peg on which the ball is placed at the beginning of a hole.

Threeball A match where three players compete against each other, each playing his own ball.

Threesome A match where one player competes against two who are taking alternate shots.

Topping Striking the ball on its top half, causing a low, ineffectual shot.

Trap Bunker.

Waggle Back-and-forth movement of the club before swinging.

Winter rules Local rules set up to protect the course and allow players to improve the lie of their balls when the course is not in top condition.

Ordering *Sports Rules in Pictures* is easy and convenient. Just call 1-800-631-8571 or send your order to:
The Putnam Publishing Group
390 Murray Hill Parkway, Dept. B
East Rutherford, NJ 07073
Also available at your local bookstore or wherever paperbacks are sold.

		PRICE		
			U.S.	CANADA
_____	Baseball Rules in Pictures	399-51597	$7.95	$10.50
_____	Official Little League Baseball Rules in Pictures	399-51531	7.95	10.50
_____	Softball Rules in Pictures	399-51356	6.95	9.25
_____	Football Rules in Pictures	399-51479	7.95	10.50
_____	Basketball Rules in Pictures	399-51590	7.95	10.50
_____	Hockey Rules in Pictures	399-51480	7.95	10.50
_____	Amateur Wrestling Rules in Pictures	399-51589	7.95	10.50
_____	Volleyball Rules in Pictures	399-51537	7.95	10.50
_____	Golf Rules in Pictures	399-51438	7.95	10.50
_____	Tennis Rules and Techniques in Pictures	399-51674	7.95	10.50
_____	Track and Field Rules in Pictures	399-51620	7.95	10.50
_____	Gymnastics Rules in Pictures	399-51636	7.95	10.50
_____	Soccer Rules in Pictures	399-51647	7.95	10.50
_____	Golf Techniques in Pictures	399-51664	7.95	10.50

Subtotal	$_____
*Postage & Handling	$_____
Sales Tax	$_____
(CA, NJ, NY, PA)	
Total Amount Due	$_____
Payable in U.S. Funds	
(No cash orders accepted)	

*Postage & Handling: $1.00 for 1 book, 25¢ for each additional book up to a maximum of $3.50.

Please send me the titles I've checked above. Enclosed is my:

☐ check   ☐ money order

Please charge my:

☐ Visa   ☐ MasterCard   ☐ American Express

Card # _____ Expiration date _____

Signature as on charge card _____

Name _____

Address _____

City _____ State _____ Zip _____

Please allow six weeks for delivery. Prices subject to change without notice.